JOSEPH SMITH'S
NEW YORK
REPUTATION
REEXAMINED

JOSEPH SMITH'S NEW YORK REPUTATION REEXAMINED

Rodger I. Anderson

SALT LAKE CITY

1990

With grateful love to my wife, Wilma,

8 December 1943 to 18 December 1988,

for adding the sweet measure of her soul to my existence.

94 93 92 91 90   4 3 2 1

Cover Design: Randall Smith Associates

Library of Congress Cataloging-in-Publication Data

Anderson, Rodger I.
    Joseph Smith's New York reputation reexamined / Rodger
I. Anderson.
        p.   cm.
    Bibliography: p.
    Includes index.
    ISBN 0-941214-81-8
    1. Smith, Joseph, 1805–1844 – Public opinion. 2. Public opinion –
New York (State) I. Title.
BX8695.S6A69 1989
289.3'092 – dc20
    [B]   89–32697
                                                                    CIP

Contents

Chapter 1

THE ISSUES

On 1 April 1842 the *Times and Seasons*, official organ of the Nauvoo, Illinois, based Church of Jesus Christ of Latter-day Saints, published another chapter in the serialized history of its founder and prophet, Joseph Smith. In this latest installment, the thirty-six-year-old Smith publicly recounted his adolescence during the 1820s in western New York, including the admission that as a youth, "I was left to all kinds of temptations, and mingling with all kinds of society, I frequently fell into many foolish errors and displayed the weakness of youth and the corruption of human nature, which I am sorry to say led me into divers temptations, to the gratification of many appetites offensive in the sight of God."[1]

The spiritual leader of some 20,000 Mormons worldwide, Smith did not cite specific offenses in his confession, an oversight his more vocal critics were only too eager to correct. According to them, at the same time Smith was receiving his first revelations during the 1820s, which would eventually lead to his founding the Mormon church on 6 April 1830, he was also deceiving credulous neighbors by pretending to see buried treasure in the earth and was notorious throughout the frontier New York community as a drunkard, blasphemer, and cheat. Not content with branding him a moral incompetent, these critics attempted to prove him a willful fraud, a confidence man who was perpetrating one of the great hoaxes of modern times. Discovering that he could dupe the unwary by claiming magical powers, they alleged, Smith turned his questionable talents to religion, where he could exploit the superstitious on a truly grand scale. Through one fabrication after another, according to detractors, he finally succeeded in organizing a church, whose primary purpose was to bring wealth to its founder.

Those who continue to view Joseph Smith in this decidedly negative light have traditionally depended upon the efforts of Doctor Philastus Hurlbut, a one-time Mormon who was excommunicated in 1833 for, among other offenses, saying "that he deceived Joseph Smith's God, or the spirit by which he was actuated."[2] Convinced that Mormonism was a deception, Hurlbut offered his services to an anti-Mormon group based in the Kirtland, Ohio, area interested in investigating rumors about Smith's early life and the possibly fraudulent origin of Smith's new scripture, the Book of Mormon. To accomplish this end, they sent Hurlbut to Palmyra, New York, where Smith had spent most of his youth and early manhood. There Hurlbut collected the signatures of over eighty people testifying to the allegedly bad character of the Smith family and of Joseph Smith in particular.

In affidavit after affidavit the young Smith was depicted as a liar and self-confessed fraud, a cunning and callous knave who delighted in nothing so much as preying upon the credulity of his neighbors. A money digger by profession, Smith spent his nights digging for treasure and his days lounging about the local grocery store entertaining his fellow tipplers with tales of midnight enchantments and bleeding ghosts, the affidavits maintained.[3]

Once published in 1834 Hurlbut's affidavits became especially dangerous to the newly founded church and its leader. To defuse the potentially explosive documents, Smith read them aloud at public meetings, denouncing them as the work of Satan. More importantly, Hurlbut's affidavits stimulated Smith to publish the first official history of the new church, "Early Scenes and Incidents in the Church," authored by Smith's closest associate at the time, Oliver Cowdery. Just as Hurlbut had revealed the "real" Joseph Smith, so Cowdery's "History" revealed another "real" Joseph Smith—though without supporting affidavits. Rather than a moral leper, Cowdery's Joseph Smith was simply a man like other men "and liable, without the assisting grace of the Savior, to deviate from that perfect path in which *all* men are commanded to walk."[4]

Hurlbut's witnesses remembered Smith as "entirely destitute of *moral character, and addicted to vicious habits.*"[5] The only sins of Cowdery's Smith "were a light, and too often, vain mind, exhibiting a foolish and trifling conversation."[6] Hurlbut's Smith was animated by no loftier purpose than the love of money, but Cowdery's Smith was in contrast motivated by a sincere desire "to know for himself of the certainty and reality of pure and holy religion."[7] Hurlbut's Smith was a money digger who told marvelous tales of enchanted treasure and infernal spirits, but Cowdery's Smith had only "*heard* of the power of enchantement, and a thousand like stories, which held the hidden treasures of the earth."[8]

Oliver Cowdery's "History" was the first, but by no means the last, attempt by Mormon writers to discredit Hurlbut's scandalous allegations. In 1881 two leading elders of the Reorganized Church of Jesus Christ of Latter

Day Saints (founded in 1860), brothers William and E. L. Kelley, interviewed a number of old Palmyra-Manchester, New York, residents in order to, in the Kelleys' words, " 'beard the lion in his den,' and hear the worst, let it hurt whom it would."[9] According to the published report of their efforts, the Kelleys could find virtually no one who knew anything firsthand against the Smiths and a number who remembered the family as being quite respectable. The worst the Kelleys could report was one account of money digging and an occasional reference to Joseph Smith's drinking.

Non-Mormons were no less zealous in collecting additional information about the young Mormon prophet. In 1880 Frederic G. Mather published an article in *Lippincott's Magazine* entitled "The Early Days of Mormonism." Mather had visited not only Palmyra but also central Pennsylvania, where Joseph Smith lived and worked for some time before the Book of Mormon appeared in late March 1830. Like Hurlbut, Mather found many people willing to talk about the young man who, in the words of one, "did not look as if he knew enough to fool people so."[10] And like Hurlbut, Mather heard stories of gold digging and drinking, although many of these same witnesses also considered Smith "a good and kind neighbor."[11] Later in the 1880s Arthur Buel Deming also acted the sleuth, publishing the results of his investigations in a short-lived, two-issue newspaper bearing the lurid title *Naked Truths About Mormonism*. Deming's results were also unlike those of the Kelleys, for he encountered no difficulty in finding people who claimed firsthand knowledge of the Smiths. Deming's informants willingly repeated all that Hurlbut's witnesses had charged over half a century before, even adding a number of new accusations to the growing list.

Together with other, widely scattered recollections and statements, these four sources—Hurlbut, the

Kelleys, Mather, and Deming—contain almost everything that is known about the young Joseph Smith from non-Mormon sources. Despite the obvious importance of these testimonials, few contemporary scholars have investigated their reliability as primary documents. Non-Mormons generally have been content to reject reports favorable to Smith on the grounds of obvious prejudice, and those sympathetic to the Saints and their church have similarly rejected testimony portraying Smith in an unfavorable light.

Occasionally, some have attempted to evaluate the reports themselves. When it first became known that Isaac Hale, Joseph Smith's father-in-law, had written a letter condemning his son-in-law as an imposter, one of Smith's early supporters, Martin Harris, responded by calling Hale's letter a forgery because "Hale was old and blind and not capable of writing it."[12] William R. Hine, who knew Hale, challenged Harris, saying that "Hale was called the greatest hunter on the Susquehanna, and two years before had killed a black deer and a white bear, which many hunters had tried to kill, also that he was intelligent and knew the Scriptures."[13] Faced with such conflicting testimony, Eber D. Howe wrote to Hale directly, reporting the charge and requesting that Hale attest his letter before a magistrate. "I hope no one has attempted to deceive us," Howe wrote, "deception and falsehood in the business will do no good in the end, but will help build up the monstrous delusion."[14] Hale responded by affirming his affidavit before a justice of the peace. He included testimonials to his veracity and an affidavit from his minister attesting that though old and occasionally requiring the use of an amanuensis, Hale yet "retains his sight and is still capable of writing."[15]

As the most ambitious attempt to disprove Hurlbut's affidavits, the Kelley interviews proved to be just as disappointing. At least three of those interviewed were so incensed with the published report that they produced affidavits of their own charging the Kelleys with misrepresentation. Among them was John H. Gilbert, who on 12 July 1881 appeared before Justice M. C. Finley and made the following deposition: "John H. Gilbert of Palmyra, Wayne county, N.Y., being duly sworn deposes and says, that in the article published in 'The Saints' Herald,' at Plano, Ill., June 1, 1881, purporting to give an interview with him on the subject of Mormonism &c., signed by Wm. H. Kelley, he is grossly misrepresented in almost every particular, words being put into his mouth that he never uttered, and the answers to questions he did give, totally at variance from the answers given by him, and as he believes, designedly."[16]

Faced with the questionable reliability of the Kelley report and the lack of credible testimony discounting the affidavits collected by Hurlbut and others, most scholars outside of Mormonism have tended to accept the non-Mormon side of the issue. The number of witnesses, the unanimity of their testimony, the failure to impeach even a single witness, and the occasional candid reminiscence by Martin Harris, Brigham Young, Joseph Smith, Lucy Mack Smith, William Smith, Joseph Knight, or other early Mormons have contributed to the conclusion that Hurlbut and his followers were probably reliable reporters. Even those who suspected that the witnesses against Smith may have been motivated by more than a simple desire to inform have not questioned the depictions of Smith as a basically self-seeking charlatan.[17]

In 1961 and 1970 two notable Mormon efforts were launched to discredit the Smith family neighbors. The first, Hugh Nibley's *The Myth Makers*, was a book-length attempt to prove that the witnesses against Joseph Smith "told the best stories they could think of, without particularly caring whether they were true or not."[18] The second and more substantial effort was a lengthy article by Richard L. Anderson entitled, "Joseph Smith's New York Reputation Reappraised."[19] In it Anderson argued that Hurlbut and Deming infected their reports with their own animosity and that their witnesses really knew very little about Joseph Smith. Anderson found the Kelley report more reliable, both because of the Kelleys' superior objectivity and because the witnesses they contacted who actually claimed to know the Smiths praised rather than condemned the family. Since the witnesses who knew Joseph Smith best were most positive in their opinions of him, Anderson argued, it follows that the most reliable authorities on the early life of Joseph Smith are members of Smith's own family.

Many Mormons have since accepted the arguments advanced by Nibley and Anderson, declaring the matter settled. Hurlbut's testimonials, explained one Mormon historian, are significant only as evidence of how "suspicious, sensitive critics reacted to Joseph's testimony by manufacturing a variety of preposterous myths." Another noted that any of Hurlbut's sources after the appearance of Anderson's article "must now be seriously questioned."[20]

Unfortunately, there has been little effort to reexamine the influential works of Nibley and Anderson to discover whether their arguments are equal to their conclusions. The following study attempts to fill this void. I believe that the testimonials collected by Hurlbut, Deming, and others are in fact largely immune to the attacks launched against them by Nibley, Anderson, and others. Hurlbut's witnesses may not have left history "of the purest ray serene," but there can be no doubt that these reports, in early twentieth-century German historian Eduard Meyer's words, "give us the general opinion of his [Smith's] neighbors in their true, essential form."[21] Whether or not it follows that the conclusions of the Smiths' neighbors about the events they witnessed are in fact justified is a task I leave to other researchers. In the meantime, it is clear that a broader picture of Joseph Smith emerges from these early affidavits and interviews than is otherwise available from family and followers.

NOTES

1. Joseph Smith's confession was originally recorded in the *Times and Seasons* 3 (April 1842): 749. An amended version, denying any inference of serious wrongdoing on the part of Smith, later appeared in Joseph Smith et al., *History of the Church of Jesus Christ of Latter-day Saints*, ed. B. H. Roberts, 6 vols. (Salt Lake City: Deseret News, 1902–12), 1:9–10.

2. *Times and Seasons* 6 (Feb. 1845): 785. Hurlbut had earlier been disfellowshipped from the church for using obscene language in the presence of young women.

3. These affidavits, among others, were first published by Eber D. Howe as part of his book, *Mormonism Unvailed* . . . (Painesville, OH: Printed and published by the author, 1834).

4. *Messenger and Advocate* 1 (Dec. 1834): 40. This and note 6 are from a letter written by Smith to introduce Cowdery's history.

5. Statement dated Palmyra, 4 Dec. 1833, Howe, 261. This statement was signed by fifty-one residents of Palmyra.

6. *Messenger and Advocate* 1 (Dec. 1834): 40.

7. Ibid. (Feb. 1835): 78.

8. Ibid. 2 (Oct. 1835): 198, emphasis mine.

9. William H. Kelley, "The Hill Cumorah . . . The Stories of Hurlbert, Howe, Tucker, &c. from Late Interviews," *Saints' Herald* 28 (1 June 1881): 162. The following year Mormon writer George Reynolds quoted at length from the Kelley interviews (though without acknowledging the *Saints' Herald*) in an article for the Mormon church's *Juvenile Instructor* (1 Oct. 1882), entitled "Joseph Smith's Youthful Life." "Joseph was undoubtedly not perfect," Reynolds noted, "none of us are—but he was far superior in almost every respect to his neighbors and associates" (p. 299).

10. *Lippincott's Magazine* 26 (1880): 199.

11. Ibid., 201.
12. Statement of W. R. Hine, see *Naked Truths about Mormonism* 1 (Jan. 1888): 2.
13. Ibid.
14. *The Susquehanna* (PA) *Register*, 1 May 1834.
15. Ibid. The affidavit of Nathaniel Lewis, Hale's minister, was also attested by W. M. Thompson, who testified that Lewis was "a man of veracity, and good moral character."
16. Copied from the original on file in the Ontario County, New York, Clerk's Office. Gilbert's statement, among others, was first published in *The Ontario County Times* (Canandaigua, NY), 27 July 1881, and later in the *Cadillac* (MI) *Weekly News*. See the undated clipping from that paper in the archives of the Reorganized Church of Jesus Christ of Latter Day Saints, Independence, Missouri.
17. J. H. Kennedy, *Early Days of Mormonism* . . . (New York: Charles Scribner's Sons, 1888), 17–18.
18. Hugh Nibley, *The Myth Makers* (Salt Lake City: Bookcraft, 1961), 6.
19. Richard L. Anderson, "Joseph Smith's New York Reputation Reappraised," *Brigham Young University Studies* 10 (Spring 1970): 283–314. Anderson has dealt with later money-digging episodes in Smith's life in an article entitled "The Mature Joseph Smith and Treasure Seeking," *Brigham Young University Studies* 24 (Fall 1984): 489–560. Because this recent article falls outside the scope of the present study, I will not treat it in what follows. Readers are nonetheless advised to approach Anderson's analysis in light of what is said hereafter about the Smiths and money digging. Considering the degree of family involvement with the seeking of hidden treasure by occult means, later events would most naturally be interpreted as continuing expressions of the same interest.
20. Milton V. Backman, Jr., *Joseph Smith's First Vision* . . . (Salt Lake City: Bookcraft, 1971), 116; Marvin S. Hill, "Brodie Revisited: A Reappraisal," *Dialogue: A Journal of Mormon Thought* 7 (Winter 1972): 77. Perhaps the most candid response from a Mormon scholar came from Richard L. Bushman, a

sympathetic biographer of Joseph Smith, who wrote in 1984, "The affidavits have been challenged for their authenticity because of Hurlbut's and Howe's undisguised animosity, but while questionable in detail, there is little reason to believe the [Palmyra-Manchester] neighbors felt otherwise." *Joseph Smith and the Beginnings of Mormonism* (Urbana: University of Illinois Press, 1984), 190.

21. Heinz F. Rahde and Eugene Seaich, trans., *The Origin and History of the Mormons* . . . (Salt Lake City: University of Utah, n.d.), 4.

Chapter 2

THE MYTH MAKERS

The fundamental argument of Hugh Nibley, one of contemporary Mormonism's leading scholars, presented in his 1961 classic response to Mormon detractors, *The Myth Makers*, is a simple one. According to Nibley, "The whole structure of anti-Mormon scholarship rests on trumped-up evidence."[1] Everywhere in these unfriendly sources he found exaggeration, pretended knowledge, prevarication, and "intrinsically absurd and thoroughly conflicting [stories]."[2] In fact, Nibley argues, these qualities infect the whole body of non-Mormon literature from Doctor Philastus Hurlbut to the present. Joseph Smith's neighbors, he concludes, were simply "a pack of story-tellers who have been getting away with too much for too long."[3]

Although praised by some as a long-needed exposé of anti-Mormonism, Nibley's work unfortunately suffers from serious failings. Its errors are many, but a number stand out because of their ubiquity. First is the unqualified scope of its generalization. Because he found *some* writers who were less than careful with the truth,

Nibley concluded that *all* such writers must have been similarly careless, a conclusion which is simply not justified.[4] Nor does it follow that because a writer errs in one place, his or her whole account is for that reason erroneous.

For example, John C. Bennett's seminal 1842 anti-Mormon book, *The History of the Saints; or, An Expose of Joe Smith and Mormonism,*[5] is most certainly unreliable in places, but it is equally certain that the book—written by a former counselor in Joseph Smith's first presidency—is not the jumble of lies some have assumed. Subsequent research has confirmed much of what appeared at the time as apostate slander. Nibley, however, does not consider that a witness whose veracity is not always absolute could ever tell the truth. Ironically, Nibley's position is logically identical to that of anti-Mormon writers who claim that Joseph Smith always prevaricated because his accounts of his first vision sometimes differ from one another or because he repeatedly denied that he ever practiced polygamy.

Also among *The Myth Makers*'s failings is its author's use of arguments which are *non sequiturs.* For example, Nibley argues at some length that the stories about Joseph Smith's money digging could be attributed to earlier money-digging stories involving other people. Since *"every* weird detail of the stories later attached to Joseph Smith is found in full bloom *before* Smith," Nibley contends that those who attribute similar stories to Smith are simply "trying to dress Joseph Smith in other men's clothes."[6] Such a conclusion not only far outstrips the available evidence, ignoring numerous contemporary witnesses who either saw Smith digging or heard him talk about the subject, it simply confirms that the practice of money digging did not originate with Smith. All it answers is the question of where Smith learned how to dig for money.

Long before Joseph Smith's neighbors alleged that he hunted for buried money by occult means, the art of magical treasure hunting was widespread in America.[7] Accounts of men pursuing enchanted treasures with divining rods are especially prevalent throughout the eighteenth century and suggest that the practice had become ritualized very early on. The buried treasure was located by a divining rod and immobilized by charms, magic circles, or special steel rods driven into the ground. Incantations were recited to protect the diggers from "certain malicious Demons who are said to hunt and guard such Places." Any deviation from the prescribed rituals on the part of the treasure hunters spoiled their chances of recovering the trove; any "Mistake in the Procedure, some rash Word spoken, or some Rule of Art neglected, the Guardian Spirit had Power to sink it deeper into the Earth and convey it out of their reach."[8]

The relevance of such practices to Nibley's hypothesis needs little comment. If by the time Joseph Smith became interested in buried money there already existed an entire lore of magical treasure hunting, then parallels of the type adduced by Nibley prove only that Smith followed approved methods in seeking elusive treasures. Without evidence of "borrowing" from other accounts there is no reason to suppose that Smith was being confused with other money diggers simply because all drew from the same complex body of occult beliefs.

Other examples of *The Myth Makers*'s lack of sound arguments include the claim that the witnesses against Smith are entirely too many and that the testimony of a more limited number would have borne more weight because a smaller group might have known Smith better.[9] Of course Nibley could then have argued that the witnesses against Smith were entirely too few for a scamp of his alleged reputation. But in any case the premises themselves are patently false. To witness someone's acts or hear a person relate his experiences does not require profound friendship. Most people have scores of acquaintances who could testify to their character on the basis of conversations or observed acts. Certainly such acquaintances may not understand the motives behind behavior and may garble conversations when reporting, but the sum of enough persons testifying to similar acts or conversations can provide a reliable index to a person's general behavior.

Nibley is also mistaken when he charges that those who testified to Smith's character were themselves disreputable, otherwise "how could they have discovered the vices they know so much about?"[10] Witnessing a deed is not the same as committing it, and hearing a man boast of some act does not necessitate participation in it.[11] Even if it could be demonstrated that Smith's accusers were in fact involved in the same practices they related, it would not mean their testimony was for that reason suspect. Defending the accused by pointing to the imperfections of their accusers is fallacious and only serves to deflect attention from the original issue. Such an argument exonerates neither side and certainly does not prove that the person originally accused is innocent simply because his accusers do not themselves have "clean hands."

Another significant defect of Nibley's analysis is its frequent high-handedness in dealing with testimony unfavorable to Smith. Rather than consider whether similar testimony from more than one person might indicate that what they report is true, Nibley often dismisses the topic with flippant and unsupported assertions. His handling of the following testimony demonstrates this characteristic response. Hezekiah McKune testified that "in conversation with Joseph Smith Jr., he (Smith) said he was nearly equal to Jesus Christ"; Levi Lewis testified "that he heard Smith say he (Smith) was as good as Jesus Christ; — that it was as bad to injure him as it was to injure Jesus Christ"; and

Sophia Lewis testified that she "heard a conversation between Joseph Smith Jr., and the Rev. James B. Roach, in which Smith . . . said . . . that he (Smith) was as good as Jesus Christ."[12] To these statements Nibley responds, "Isn't it fairly obvious that the three cooked the story up among themselves before they went to the magistrate?"[13] Nibley's only reason for claiming this is that these three witnesses went together to make their depositions and that McKune was a "close friend" of the Lewises. Even if true, this does not necessarily prove collusion. But, in fact, no evidence even exists that McKune was on intimate terms with the Lewises, that the three were in company when they made their depositions, or that they had met together and discussed the matter beforehand. All are details supplied by Nibley, not by the documents.

To cast further suspicion on the affidavits of the Lewises and McKune, Nibley charges exaggeration by quoting a later source alleging that Joseph Smith "was *often* heard during his lifetime to declare himself *far* superior to our Savior."[14] Nibley observes, "Well, you see how these things grow. First Mr. McKune in 1834 says that Smith claimed he was '*nearly* equal' to Jesus; then the Lewises improved on that—each of them heard Smith say he was '*as good* as Jesus Christ;' finally in 1851 it is remembered that he 'was *often* heard . . . to declare himself *far superior* to our Savior.' "[15] Again, Nibley's charge is without foundation. The assertion that McKune preceded the Lewises in testifying is not corroborated by evidence. Further, if the three are testifying to separate experiences, as Nibley seems to believe, their variation in language is insignificant. Finally, the late source adduced by Nibley as proving "how these things grow" may simply prove that the author of the article was careless in his reporting or reflect the recollection of a different statement altogether. Despite this,

Nibley insists that if the latter article exaggerates, then McKune and the Lewises must surely have exaggerated too.

This charge of exaggerated hearsay occurs repeatedly throughout Nibley's book. For example, he accuses John Hyde of embroidering Barton Stafford's account of having seen Joseph Smith drunk in a hay field. According to Nibley, Hyde's statement that Smith "when drunk . . . would talk about his religion"[16] goes beyond what Stafford actually said, which was that Smith got into a drunken fight while working for his father. However, in his original statement Stafford concluded: "As an evidence of his [Smith's] piety and devotion, when intoxicated, he frequently made his religion the topic of conversation!!"[17] Thus Hyde and Stafford agree, with Nibley failing to quote Stafford in full.

Nibley further misrepresents the issue of Joseph Smith's drinking when he introduces the recollection of a witness who supposedly saw Smith lying drunk in a field during the summer of 1844.[18] Nibley quotes this recollection, attributing it to C. C. Weil,[19] and then remarks about "how these things grow" and refers to Weil's "improvement" on Hyde's "improvement" of Stafford's original statement.[20] Nibley does not explain how Weil, whose account was printed in 1854, could "improve" on Hyde's account, which was not published until 1857, nor does he explain how Weil's experience, which supposedly occurred in 1844 at Montrose, Iowa, is an embellishment of Stafford's experience, which occurred sometime during the late 1820s in Manchester, New York. The two stories share neither time, place, nor general circumstances. Yet Nibley assumes a genetic-like relationship between the accounts simply because both refer to Smith drunk in a field. If Smith, as so many contemporaries alleged, was given to occasional bouts with the bottle, he could have been seen intoxicated in sim-

ilar situations on more than one occasion. Smith's enthusiasm for wine and beer up to the time of his death in 1844
certainly lends credibility to these earlier stories.[21]

The Myth Makers is also marred by numerous factual errors. Nibley claims, for example, that some of
Philastus Hurlbut's witnesses later "went back" on their
1833–34 testimony and that when interviewed years later
"spoke very well of Smith, and had nothing bad whatever
to say about him."[22] Of Hurlbut's many witnesses, only
one was interviewed years later by William and E. L. Kelley,
and he reaffirmed his original testimony. Abel Chase, who
in 1833 joined ten others in signing an affidavit charging
the Smiths with indolence, intemperance, and untrustworthi-
ness, told the Kelleys in 1881 that the Smith family was
superstitious, shiftless, and untrustworthy. Chase did not
mention intemperance, but the Kelleys apparently did not
ask Chase about this charge. From other interviews, the
Kelleys did find that the drinking habits of the Smiths were
not different from those of their neighbors, although one
neighbor recalled Joseph Smith and his father getting drunk
on one occasion.

Nibley's use of the Kelley interviews introduces
another failing: a tendency to suppress information potentially harmful to traditional interpretations of the Mormon
past. For example, Nibley was aware that the Kelleys' report was challenged only days after its original publication, but he ignores the fact, presumably because this information would undermine his contention that some of
Hurlbut's witnesses reneged on their original testimonies.

Nibley's suppression of vital information in this
instance seems intentional. For on the same pages of the
source he cites to prove his points, Charles A. Shook's *The
True Origin of Mormon Polygamy*,[23] appear affidavits chal-
lenging the accuracy of the Kelley report. These Nibley trans-
mutes into a vague statement that the purported denials of

the Hurlbut witnesses were not "unanimous." Without a copy of Shook's work at hand, the reader has no way of knowing that the retractions to which Nibley alludes were made in reference to the Kelley report, not the testimonials collected by Hurlbut.

Still another of *The Myth Makers*'s many problems is a lack of scholarly standards in evaluating sources. Firsthand accounts are impeached because they are not consistent with anti-Mormon fulminations of a century later, and contemporary accounts of episodes in Joseph Smith's life are discredited almost wholly on the basis of later secondary reports. For example, in discussing the "mighty band" of diggers employed by Smith in hunting treasure, Nibley cites fifteen sources, only three of which pretend to have known Smith during the time he was hunting for buried treasures. Smith's digging techniques are treated similarly, for of the six disparate sources cited by Nibley, only one pretends to be an eyewitness account. The rest are imaginative reconstructions found in books published from 1851 to 1920, not one of which contains any personal recollections of Smith by firsthand witnesses.

By thus arbitrarily increasing the number of its "witnesses," *The Myth Makers* not only impresses readers with its wide-ranging scholarship but augments the probability of finding contradictions. Nibley's success depends in large measure upon impugning one witness by citing another, disparate witness. Since the earliest accounts are not sufficiently inconsistent, Nibley depends heavily on nonwitnesses. Thus he quotes C. S. Jones as saying that a "full moon" was essential for Smith's money digging performances and O. S. Belisle as saying that Smith and his friends dug for money "when there was neither moon, nor stars to spy upon them,"[24] without mentioning that neither writer pretends to a personal knowledge of his subject. The one eyewitness to comment on this aspect of Smith's money-digging career Nibley passes by in silence, apparently unwilling to impeach a contemporary account with secondhand sources not written until decades later.

Nibley's indiscriminate use of sources enables him not only to oppose witnesses with non-witnesses but also to introduce sources whose only merit is that they make others appear unreliable by comparison. Thus in discussing the year in which Joseph Smith allegedly became a money digger, Nibley cites a book published in 1902 which dates Smith's digging to 1817. Since other sources, according to Nibley, give the year as 1819, 1820, and 1822, Nibley can now add 1817 to his list to highlight the disparity. (Nibley does not mention Joseph Smith's own contradictions in trying to remember the date as well as other specifics of his first vision.)

J. E. Mahaffey, whom Nibley quotes as a source for the 1817 date, gives as his informant an "old man" who "testifies that Smith was about this time [1817] employed to locate wells and look for gold with his 'divining rods' of witchhazel and his 'seer-stone.' "[25] Obviously a nameless "old man" remembering an incident which occurred eighty-five years before is not the most reliable witness imaginable, especially since there exists no other evidence to corroborate his story. The phrase "about this time" is hardly exact, considering the number of elapsed years. Nor does Mahaffey's witness specify that it was Joseph Smith the Mormon prophet who was the subject of his recollection. It is known that there was another man named Smith operating in the same area around 1815 and that this Smith was also an oracle and money digger.[26] Without knowing which Smith the old man had in mind, this recollection is of questionable value even if true.

Besides quoting Mahaffey's witness, Nibley also cites J. H. Kennedy as stating that Smith's first venture as a money digger was in 1819, Pomeroy Tucker as stating that it occurred in 1820, and Willard Chase as claiming that it "was not until 1822 or after."[27] Kennedy was in fact a biographer of Smith, not a witness of his money digging, and depended for his date on Pomeroy Tucker's earlier account. Nibley paraphrases Kennedy as saying that Smith "started looking for treasures with a peep-stone" in 1819. What Kennedy actually said, following Tucker, who knew Smith personally, was that the stone was *found* in 1819 but not used by Smith for money digging until 1820. Thus to derive his contradiction, Nibley misquotes Kennedy, who was simply following Tucker's account, and then quotes Tucker to oppose the two as irreconcilable.

Also, Chase did not say, as Nibley intimates, that Smith did not dig for money until "1822 or after" but rather that after obtaining a stone from Chase in 1822, Smith made such a disturbance in the community that Chase ordered the stone returned. Chase explicitly says that this did not mark the beginning of Smith's money digging, which he, agreeing with Tucker, assigns to the year 1820.[28] Thus of the four sources cited by Nibley as disagreeing about the year of Smith's first money-digging venture, one is untrustworthy and the other three are in harmony.

Another of Nibley's errors is a failure to consider Mormon sources when they concur with non-Mormon accounts. Nibley makes light of non-Mormon claims that the Book of Mormon was originally discovered by the same means Joseph Smith claimed to use for locating buried treasures, but he chooses to ignore Martin Harris's statement of 1859: "Joseph . . . described the manner of finding his plates. He found them by looking in the stone found in the well of Mason Chase. The family had likewise told me the same thing."[29] Harris, who was the first convert to Mormonism outside the Smith family, here confirms Orsamus Turner's 1851 recollection that the Smith family "said it was by looking at this stone in a hat, the light excluded, that

Joseph discovered the plates."[30] Nibley ignores Harris's statement, for to do otherwise would lend an air of respectability to one of those sources Nibley condemns as "beneath notice."

The Myth Makers also tends to disregard context. In his eagerness to impugn the whole *corpus* of non-Mormon literature, Nibley misquotes, misphrases, and misrepresents his opponents. For example, he has Orsamus Turner state that the only "peep-stone" Smith ever used was the Urim and Thummin found with the plates. However, Turner states not only that the plates were found by means of a stone but also that it was "the same stone the Smiths had used in money digging, and in some pretended discoveries of stolen property."[31] Not only does Nibley quote, in several places, from Turner's entire report, in one place he quotes from the very paragraph in which Turner writes about Smith's peep-stone. On that occasion, however, Nibley attributes the remark not to Turner but to G. W. Cowles, who reprinted Turner's account verbatim in his *Landmarks of Wayne County New York*.[32] Why Nibley does this is unclear, unless he does not want readers to know that his source is the same in both instances.[33]

Nibley's misrepresentation is manifest even when he is accusing others of the same mistake. For example, he refers to Pomeroy Tucker's account of Joseph Smith's first money-digging venture and quotes Tucker as saying that "several of the individuals participating in this, and many others well remembering the stories of the time, are yet living witness of these follies. . . . " Nibley claims he has thus caught Tucker describing witnesses, "not of the events, but of 'the *stories* of the time.' "[34] But Tucker's entire statement reads: "This was the inauguration of the impostor's money-digging performances; and the description given of this first trial and of its results is as near exactitude as can at this time be recollected from his own accounts. Several

of the individuals participating in this and subsequent diggings, and many others well remembering the stories of
the time, are yet living witnesses of these follies, and can
make suitable corrections if the particulars as stated are not
substantially according to the facts."[35] Clearly, then, the
phrase "living witnesses" refers primarily to "individuals
participating in this and subsequent diggings" and only par-
enthetically to those "remembering the stories of the time."
Of the three sources of information listed by Tucker, Nibley
seizes on the least significant as if it were Tucker's only
claim to credence.

Finally, Nibley's method of analysis is arbitrary.
The same method applied to the "traditional" Mormon history would easily result in equal confusion. Using Nibley's
same criteria, it would be easy to demonstrate the intrinsic
contradictions in the canonized account of Mormon origins,
pointing to various improbable stories, exaggerations, and
every other shortcoming Nibley heaps on non-Mormons.

Thus Nibley's *The Myth Makers* only proves what
no one ever thought of denying, namely that not all historical documents are of the same evidential quality. Beyond
that rather obvious fact, Nibley's argument fails on every
significant point. Illogic, unsupported speculation, specious
charges, misrepresentation, factual errors, indiscriminate and
arbitrary use of sources, disregard of context, and a lack of
scholarly standards characterize the book advertised by its
publisher as a "masterful expose . . . [of] the makers of
myths who told their untruths about Joseph Smith."[36]

If Joseph Smith's neighbors are to be discredited,
it must be on the basis of better evidence than that advanced
by Nibley.

NOTES

1. Hugh Nibley, *The Myth Makers* (Salt Lake City: Bookcraft, 1961), 5.
2. Ibid., 189.
3. Ibid., 6.
4. Among the numerous examples to the contrary which might be listed are John Corrill's *A Brief History of the Church of Christ of Latter Day Saints* . . . (St. Louis: Printed for the author, 1839); T. B. H. Stenhouse's *The Rocky Mountain Saints* . . . (New York: D. Appleton and Company, 1873); John D. Lee's *Mormonism Unveiled* . . . (St. Louis: Bryan, Brand & Co., 1877); and William Wyl, *Mormon Portraits* . . . (Salt Lake City: Tribune Printing & Publishing Company, 1886).
5. John C. Bennett, *The History of the Saints; or, An Expose of Joe Smith and Mormonism* (Boston: Leland & Whiting, 1842).
6. Nibley, 190, 183.
7. For an excellent survey of pre-Joseph Smith money digging in America, see Herbert Leventhal's *In the Shadow of the Enlightenment: Occultism and Renaissance Science in Eighteenth-Century America* (New York: New York University Press, 1976), 110–18. For Joseph Smith's and other early Mormons' direct involvement, see D. Michael Quinn, *Early Mormonism and the Magic World View* (Salt Lake City: Signature Books, 1986). Contemporary references to money digging include the *Palmyra Herald*, 24 July 1822; the *Ontario Repository*, 9 Feb. 1825; the Palmyra *Wayne Sentinel*, 16 Feb. and 27 Dec. 1825; the Vermont *Rutland Herald*, 22 Aug. 1826; the *Lyons Advertizer*, 29 Aug. 1827; the *Vermont American*, 7 May 1828; the New York *Norwich Journal*, 2 July 1828; the Rochester *Gem*, 15 May 1830; the *Palmyra Reflector*, 1 Feb. 1831; Thurlow Weed, *Life* . . . 2 vols. (Boston: Houghton, Mifflin and Company, 1883–84), 1:7; and Barnes Frisbie, *The History of Middleton, Vermont* . . . (Rutland, VT: Tuttle & Co., Printers, 1867), 43–64. This last source also presents tentative evidence that Joseph Smith, Sr., before Joseph Jr.'s birth, was involved in a short-lived religious cult which advocated among other notions belief in divining rods, which if true would explain occasional references to the elder

Smith's money digging before his famous son's involvement. This cult, which broke up around 1802, also listed among its more prominent members William Cowdery, Oliver Cowdery's father, who appears to have brought up his children in the same faith. When Oliver Cowdery first met Joseph Smith in 1829, Smith praised his convert's "gift of working with the rod: behold it has told you things: behold there is no other power save God, that can cause this rod of nature, to work in your hands." *A Book of Commandments* . . . (Zion: W. W. Phelps & Co., 1833), 19. Later Smith reworded this statement, obscuring the exact nature of Cowdery's "gift."

8. *The American Weekly Mercury*, 27 March 1729, in Leonard W. Labaree et al., eds., *The Papers of Benjamin Franklin* (New Haven: Yale University Press, 1959–), 1:137. Franklin's entire article should be read as evidence of how widespread the practice had become by 1729.

9. Nibley, 29.

10. Ibid., 17.

11. Nibley points to the repeated claim that these neighbors were "intimately acquainted" with Smith, forgetting that such a claim is an editorial comment and not part of their original testimonies. Later writers stressed the intimate friendship between Smith and his neighbors for effect, but few of the actual witnesses claimed more than a fairly extended acquaintance. This may indeed limit the value of their testimony but not because they were "pretty low-life themselves."

12. Howe, 268, 269. These statements, among others, first appeared in the *Susquehanna Register*, 1 May 1834, and the *Baptist Register*, 13 June 1834, before being reprinted by Howe.

13. Nibley, 37.

14. "The Yankee Majomet," *American Whig Review* 7 (June 1851): 559; Nibley's emphasis.

15. Nibley, 36–37.

16. John Hyde, *Mormonism: Its Leaders and Designs* (New York: W. P. Fetridge & Company, 1857), 246.

17. Howe, 251.

18. *The Californian Crusoe* . . . (London: John Henry Parker, 1854), 84.

19. The actual author is unknown. From the text it appears that Robert Richards wrote the book, but this may be a pseudonym.

20. Nibley, 14.

21. See Scott H. Faulring, ed., *An American Prophet's Record: The Diaries and Journals of Joseph Smith* (Salt Lake City: Signature Books, 1987), 105, 117, 153–54, 294, 375, 486,

22. Nibley, 28.

23. Charles A. Shook, *The True Origin of Mormon Polygamy* (Cincinnati: The Standard Publishing Company, 1914).

24. C. Sheridan Jones, *The Truth about the Mormons* . . . (London: William Rider & Son, Ltd., 1920), 11; Orvilla S. Belisle, *The Prophets; or Mormonism Unveiled* (Philadelphia: Wm. White Smith, 1855), 19.

25. *Found at Last! Positive Proof that Mormonism is a Fraud and the Book of Mormon a Fable* . . . (Augusta, GA: Chronicle Job Office, 1902), 14.

26. The Rochester *Gem*, 15 May 1830.

27. Nibley, 112.

28. Howe, 240. Tucker's and Chase's accounts do disagree on another point, but not about the year in which Smith began digging for money. Tucker states that Smith borrowed Chase's stone in 1819, but Chase says that Smith procured it from him in 1822. Tucker should in this instance be rejected in favor of Chase, who is not only an earlier and more careful witness but also was there and speaks from firsthand experience. Unfortunately, when Tucker wrote his book, Chase was paralyzed and thus incapable of correcting the error.

29. *Tiffany's Monthly* 5 (Aug. 1859): 169.

30. Orsamus Turner, *History of the Pioneer Settlement of Phelps and Gorham's Purchase* . . . (Rochester: Erastus Darrow, Publisher, 1851), 216.

31. Ibid.

32. Nibley, 118; G. W. Cowles, *Landmarks of Wayne County New York* (Syracuse, NY: D. Mason & Company, Publishers, 1895).

33. Nibley, 123.
34. Ibid., 91.
35. Pomeroy Tucker, *The Origin, Rise, and Progress of Mormonism* (New York: D. Appleton and Co., 1867), 22.
36. This is from the jacket of the 1979 Bookcraft (Salt Lake City) reissue of Nibley's book.

Chapter 3

THE HURLBUT AFFIDAVITS

PART ONE

hen Brigham Young University religion professor Richard L. Anderson's "Joseph Smith's New York Reputation Reappraised" appeared in *Brigham Young University Studies* in 1970, it provided for many readers the long-awaited scholarly answer to "Hurlbut's hurlings," offering evidence where others had offered only conjecture.[1] "Anderson's findings confirm what should have been suspected all along," one of Anderson's colleagues at BYU afterwards wrote, that "they [Hurlbut's affidavits] were at best highly colored and at worst deliberately misrepresentative accounts."[2] Hailed as a minor classic in Mormon historiography, Anderson's analysis has since been relied on as the last word in primary scholarship on the subject of Joseph Smith's New York reputation.[3]

Superior as it is to Nibley's analysis in method and scholarly apparatus, Anderson's article still falls short on several counts. Its errors may be summarized under three main headings: misrepresentation of the contents and circumstances surrounding the compilation of the affidavits; failure to consider alternative interpretations for the evidence; and invalid conclusions based on faulty premises. In Anderson's analysis these errors recur regularly and sometimes flagrantly.

Anderson's first charge of substance is that Hurlbut either composed or heavily edited the depositions he collected. Anderson finds evidence of this contention in the similar structuring of the affidavits and the use of certain recurring words: "acquainted with," "entitle," "digging for money," "addicted to," "lazy," "liar," "intemperate," "pretended," "visionary," "general employment," etc. What Anderson did not mention is that other statements about Joseph Smith dating from the early 1830s, statements which Hurlbut did not collect and which are not dependent on him, display many of the same characteristics. In the Pennsylvania statements made during the same period certain words recur: "acquainted with," "pretended," "liar," "digging for," "money-diggers." In an 1833 letter written by Jesse Townsend, minister of Palmyra's Presbyterian church, the following words appear: "intemperate," "pretended," "digging for money," and "visionary." This letter is similar in structure with Hurlbut's general Palmyra statement and also with the statement of Parley Chase.[4] The structure and wording of all of these statements seem to reflect more about the period, geographic location, and level of education than an undisclosed common authorship.

Even if Hurlbut did contribute to the style and structure of the affidavits, it does not necessarily follow that he "contaminated" them by interpolation. Similarities such as those noted by Anderson may only mean that Hurlbut submitted the same questions to some of the parties involved. The question "Was digging for money the general employment of the Smith family?" repeated to each witness would explain Peter Ingersoll's "The general employment of the family, was digging for money," William

Stafford's "A great part of their time was devoted to digging for money," Parley Chase's "Digging for money was their principle employment," and David Stafford's "The general employment of the Smith family was money-digging and fortune telling."[5] This kind of question would not pass contemporary standards of opinion polling, but neither would statements gathered by Joseph Smith, including the testimonies of the witnesses to the gold plates of the Book of Mormon, for example. One must remember the time and place and disregard the polemics which colored most of the writing of the period.

Other questions which Hurlbut could have submitted include: How long were you acquainted with the Smith family? What was the general reputation of the Smiths? Was it such as to entitle them to respectability among their neighbors, or were they addicted to indolence, intemperance, or lying? Were the pretended revelations of the Smiths accepted by the community in which they lived or was the family notorious for visionary projects? Answers to questions such as these would explain all the similarities in structure and language noted by Anderson without making Hurlbut the author of the statements and only indirectly responsible for their sometimes similar phraseology.

Even if Hurlbut had written out some of the statements after interviewing those concerned, the individuals either signed the statements, thus affirming their supposed accuracy, or swore to the statements before a magistrate. For example, Peter Ingersoll appeared before Judge Thomas P. Baldwin "and made oath according to law, to the truth of the above statement." William and Barton Stafford appeared before the same judge, affirmed, and then signed their respective statements. Willard Chase and David Stafford each appeared before Frederick Smith, a local justice of the peace, and "made oath that the foregoing statement to which he has subscribed his name, is true, according to his best recollection and belief." Henry Harris similarly attested to the truthfulness of his statement before a justice of the peace, Jonathan Lapham.[6] Not all of Hurlbut's statements are in the form of affidavits, but all were signed by the respective parties as true reflections of their beliefs, and none of them ever corrected the statements or accused Hurlbut of misrepresentation.[7]

Besides these considerations, there is another which suggests that Hurlbut was not the unprincipled purveyor of false information depicted by Anderson. When Hurlbut submitted his collected statements to newspaper editor Eber D. Howe for publication, Hurlbut was embroiled in legal difficulties with Joseph Smith which made Howe suspect Hurlbut's motives. The Mormons were also denouncing Hurlbut's statements as fabrications, a charge which Howe had no way of controverting without independently verifying Hurlbut's statements. Accordingly Howe decided upon a "spot check" of Hurlbut's affidavits, hoping thereby to determine their authenticity without having to reinterview every witness. He first wrote to Isaac Hale and received in reply a long notarized statement and an affidavit from Hale's son Alva testifying that the notarized statement was "correct and true."[8] Howe then traveled to Conneaut, Ohio, to see if the statements Hurlbut had collected there accusing Smith of plagiarism in writing the Book of Mormon were authentic. While there he "saw most of the witnesses . . . and was satisfied they were not . . . mistaken in their statements."[9] Apparently this was enough to satisfy Howe of the integrity of Hurlbut's reports. He promptly published them as part of his book, *Mormonism Unvailed*.[10]

Anderson is most concerned with the general Palmyra and Manchester statements, arguing that somebody had to write them "and Hurlbut is the best candidate."[11] Granting this, however, does not mean that the statements are inaccurate reflections of their signers' intentions. Abel Chase's reaffirmation of the general Manchester statement has already been discussed, and although Chase at the time did not claim to remember much beyond "general character," he clearly did recall Smith borrowing a stone from his brother Willard, which was never returned.[12] This recollection probably formed the basis of the general statement's claim that the Smiths were men whose "word was not to be depended upon."[13]

Jesse Townsend, who on 4 December 1833 joined his name with fifty others on the general Palmyra statement, wrote a letter to Phineas Stiles on 24 December which was more strident than the collective statement. In the letter Townsend accuses Joseph Smith of being "a person of questionable character, of intemperate habits, and latterly a noted *money-digger*. . . . He has had a stone, into which, when placed in a hat, he pretended to look and see chests of money buried in the earth. He was also a *fortune teller*, and he claimed to know where stolen goods went—probably too well." Townsend describes Mormon benefactor Martin Harris as an "industrious farmer" but also a "visionary fanatic" who beat his wife and "is considered here to this day, a brute in his domestic relations, a fool and dupe to Smith in religion, and an unlearned, conceited hypocrite, generally." Townsend concluded, "I know of no one now living in this section of the country that ever gave them credence."[14]

Although more inflammatory than the general statement, the similarities between Townsend's letter and the collective Palmyra statement he signed only weeks earlier seem to confirm Hurlbut's abilities as a reporter. In that statement the Smiths are accused of being money diggers and addicted to "vicious habits"; Townsend calls them "intemperate habits." In the general statement Martin Harris is described as an honest businessman but "perfectly visionary" on the matter of religion; Townsend describes him as an "industrious farmer" but possessed of a "vision-ary mind." Finally, Townsend's observation that no one then living in the area "ever gave them credence" is re-flected in the general Palmyra report's conclusion: "we know not of a single individual in this vicinity that puts the least confidence in their pretended revelations." Such parallels in themselves do not prove anything about the character of Joseph Smith, but they do indicate that Hurlbut was prob-ably not as careless a reporter as Anderson indicates.

Anderson's second major finding is that Hurlbut's shorter affidavits contain nothing detrimental to the char-acter of Joseph Smith, especially on the charge of money digging. In reaching this conclusion, Anderson first rejects a few of the affidavits. For example, Joshua Stafford claimed that Smith showed him a piece of wood from a money box which moved under the earth and remembered that Joseph Smith had claimed to have discovered a box full of watches, but Anderson dismisses this report on the ground that Staf-ford himself was a money digger, "which renders such in-direct evidence against Joseph Smith suspect." Anderson rejects Joseph Capron's statement because Capron did not explicitly say that he observed the Smiths digging for trea-sure. He likewise discards Barton Stafford's recollection of Smith engaging in a drunken brawl because it is not clear "whether this is a story or an observation."[15]

Although Barton Stafford did not specifically say that he personally observed Joseph Smith in a drunken brawl, other members of the Stafford family also described the incident, one concluding explicitly, "I have often seen him [Joseph Smith] drunk."[16] Similarly, the fact that Joseph Capron did not say he actually saw the Smiths digging for treasure does not mean that his report contains "no per-sonal observation." As a neighbor of the Smiths, Capron was certainly in a position to know something of their ac-tivities, especially since he states that Smith "would often tell his neighbors of his wonderful discoveries, and urge them to embark in the money digging business." He also recounts a conversation with the elder Smith which clearly implicates the family in money digging.[17] Capron unfortunately is not equally clear on the source for the "fantastic dig" he so vividly describes but was at least confident enough of the story to name a confirming witness, Samuel Lawrence, whom Capron identifies as one of the chief actors in the drama. Lawrence resided in the area for many years after Howe's *Mormonism Unvailed* appeared and was consequently available to anyone who might question the truthfulness of Capron's statement.

Similarly deficient is Anderson's claim that Joshua Stafford's statement is "suspect" because Stafford had once dug for money with Smith, although he "alleges no personal observation" in his report. Considering Smith's notoriety as a money digger, it would not be surprising that Stafford was less than eager to be counted among that "selected audience of ignorant and superstitious persons" who were popularly regarded as Smith's "dupes."[18] The fact that Stafford and Smith had dug for money together also indicates that Stafford was speaking from personal knowledge when he recounted the "marvelous stories" Smith told "about ghosts, hob-goblins, caverns, and various other mysterious matters."[19] It would likewise explain why Smith asked Stafford to provide security on a horse he wanted to borrow. According to Stafford, Smith "said he would reward me handsomely, for he had found a box of watches, and they were as large as his fist, and he put one of them to his ear, and he could hear it 'tick forty rods.' " Stafford was probably one of the few people in Manchester who would seriously consider accepting such unusual collateral.

Anderson dismisses other witnesses on the ground that their statements are "limited to reported (and possibly garbled) conversations with Joseph Smith, not observations on any act of the Mormon founder."[20] Thus he rejects Henry Harris's conversation with Smith because it is "close enough to the prophet's own claims to be garbled in the telling." He impugns Roswell Nichol's exchange with Joseph Smith, Sr., on the ground that it resembles the latter's "known belief in the Book of Mormon."

It is certainly possible that Henry Harris's report could be a "garbled" account of Joseph Smith's "own claims," but Anderson neglects to mention that the only evidence we have of Smith's "own claims" from this early period from both sympathetic and unsympathetic sources supports Harris's "garbled" account in every particular. Nor does Anderson explain how Nichol's exchange with the elder Smith about money digging and the Book of Mormon can be explained on the basis of the latter's "known belief in the Book of Mormon," when Nichol expressly states that he had many conversations with Smith about money digging in which no reference was made to a "Gold Bible." In fact it was this which impressed Nichol most about one conversation, when Smith "stated their digging was . . . for the obtaining of a Gold Bible," because this so directly contradicted the earlier claims, often repeated to Nichol, that they were digging "for money."[21] Anderson also does not mention the distinct possibility that Smith's "known belief in the Book of Mormon" may have involved a belief in money digging. The Book of Mormon contains several references to "slippery" treasures capable of moving through the earth,[22] which is precisely what Hurlbut's witnesses said the Smiths had been seeking since at least 1820.

Anderson's blanket assertion that all remembered conversations are "possibly garbled" and thus inadmissible as evidence is unacceptable for several reasons. For one, without some independent reason to suspect distortion, the possibility that a conversation has been "garbled" in the remembering is no more likely than that it has been recalled accurately, especially in those cases in which a witness claims to have had a more than passing association with the subject. For another, the argument cannot explain why so many reported conversations with the Smiths should display similarly same "garbled" qualities. Knowing that a hundred people testified separately to conversations with Smith about his money digging and the "ghosts, infernal spirits, mountains of gold and silver" which he claimed to be able to see through his stone, Anderson must have considered in his own mind the possibility that the witnesses were testifying with varying degrees of accuracy to actual admissions made by Smith in conversation. Add to these supposed admissions firsthand testimonies such as that of William Stafford (discussed below), documents such as the 1826 court record wherein Smith confessed to being a "glass looker,"[23] and the fact (admitted by Smith and many of his followers) and the inadequacy of Anderson's "garbled" argument becomes apparent. More than the fallibility of human memory is needed to explain why so many individual memories should be faulty on the one particular also supported by more direct testimony.[24]

Anderson's method of dealing with reports alleging direct contact with Smith is hardly more satisfactory. For instance, he dismisses David Stafford's account of a fight he once had with Smith on the grounds that it is different from what Anderson supposes is Joseph Smith's description of the same event. According to Stafford, while he and Smith were digging a coal pit, "a dispute arose between us, (he having drinked a little too freely) and some hard words passed between us, and as usual with him at such times, was for fighting. He got the advantage of me in the scuffle, and a gentleman by the name of Ford interfered, when Joseph turned to fighting him. We both entered a complaint against him and he was fined for the breach of the Peace."[25] Anderson quotes Smith's account of what he claims is the same event: "While supper was preparing Joseph related an anecdote. While young, his father had a fine large watch dog, which bit off an ear from David Stafford's hog, which Stafford had turned into the Smith corn field. Stafford shot the dog, and with six other fellows pitched upon him unawares. And Joseph whipped the whole of them and escaped unhurt, which they swore to as recorded in Hurlburt or Howe's book." Since, Anderson concludes, "the above incident takes on such a different context in being told by Stafford or Smith, it is a striking reminder that controversial events cannot be settled by hearing only one side."[26]

Considering the differences in the two stories — one occurring at a coal pit involving three individuals, the other in a corn field involving eight people — it is likely that the two men are describing different experiences. Nevertheless, Anderson does not consider which of the two stories, if they are in fact descriptions of the same event, is the more plausible. Stafford's recollection dates from a decade earlier than Smith's and is presented in the form of a sworn affidavit, whereas Smith's is presented as a before-supper anecdote, as a rebuttal to the Stafford statement, although Smith does not seem to accurately remember the content of the Stafford account.[27] Stafford's account of the fight has Smith vanquishing two men in succession, whereas Smith presents himself as thrashing seven men simultaneously and escaping unhurt, an improbability even if allowance is made for athletic prowess. In addition, Stafford had reason to be more careful in his reporting than Smith. He not only names a witness to the incident but refers to a legal report which could have easily proven him a liar if his story did not accord with the facts. Smith, on the other hand, is far distant in time and place from the alleged event and is surrounded by loyal followers.

Anderson attempts to further discredit Stafford's

affidavit by stating that if Stafford "took his complaint to the local justice of the peace, the extant record does not show it, though it covers only the years 1827–1830."[28] According to Stafford, however, the incident took place prior to Smith's "going to Pennsylvania to get married," which occurred some time in late 1826.[29] It should come as no surprise that extant records would contain no mention of the action.

      Anderson's final point concerning Stafford's affidavit is that the surviving legal records reveal that Stafford "was plaintiff in three suits and defendant in six suits of collection, a record in the locality. With this streak of cantankerousness, one is not inclined to think that Joseph Smith was necessarily the guilty party in quarreling with David Stafford."[30] The fact that Stafford was defendant in six suits is irrelevant in determining "cantankerousness," since Stafford did not initiate the actions. The three suits initiated by Stafford pertain only to financial obligations and prove nothing concerning "quarrelsomeness." What they do prove is that Stafford was not above resorting to legal remedies for assumed wrongs. Thus it would have been in character for him to enter a complaint against Smith for "breach of the Peace."

NOTES

1. Richard L. Anderson, "Joseph Smith's New York Reputation Reappraised," *Brigham Young University Studies* 10 (Spring 1970): 283–314.
2. Marvin S. Hill, "Brodie Revisited: A Reappraisal," *Dialogue: A Journal of Mormon Thought* 7 (Winter 1972): 77.
3. For evidence of Anderson's continuing influence on the historiography of early Mormonism, see the relevant sections of James B. Allen and Glen M. Leonard, *The Story of the Latter-day Saints* (Salt Lake City: Deseret Book Company, 1976); Donna Hill, *Joseph Smith: The First Mormon* (Garden City, NY:

Doubleday & Company, Inc., 1977); Leonard J. Arrington and Davis Bitton, *The Mormon Experience . . .* (New York: Alfred A. Knopf, 1979); and Dean Jessee, "Joseph Smith's Reputation among Historians," *Ensign* 9 (Sept. 1979): 57–61. For a dissenting voice, see Wesley P. Walters, "Joseph Smith's Bainbridge, N.Y., Court Trials," *Westminster Theological Journal* 36 (Winter 1974): 152–53; and D. Michael Quinn, *Early Mormonism and the Magic World View* (Salt Lake City: Signature Books, 1987), 41–52, 125–28.

4. Townsend's letter, dated 24 December 1833, originally appeared in Pomeroy Tucker, *The Origin, Rise and Progress of Mormonism* (New York: D. Appleton and Co., 1867), 288–91. Later on 16 August 1834, Townsend wrote another letter containing essentially the same information. A copy of this second letter, clipped from an unidentified newspaper, which reprints it from the *Sacket's Harbor* (NY) *Courier*, is in the J. B. Turner collection in the Illinois State Historical Library, Springfield, Illinois.

5. Eber D. Howe, *Mormonism Unvailed . . .* (Painesville, OH: Printed and published by the author, 1834), 232, 237, 249.

6. Ibid., 237, 240, 248, 250, 251, 252.

7. This was through no lack of opportunity. Mormon missionaries periodically visited the region throughout the lifetimes of those interviewed by Hurlbut, and some of them actually went from house to house in an effort to controvert Hurlbut's witnesses. Apparently none of these efforts resulted in anything that could be used against Hurlbut, for nothing appeared in the Mormon press on the subject until the Kelleys published their doubtful report in 1881. Their failure, coupled with this almost total silence, argues in favor of Hurlbut's own statement of 1879: "All the affidavits procured by me for Mr. Howe's book, including all those from Palmyra, N.Y., were certainly genuine." Statement of D. P. Hurlbut, 19 Aug. 1879, Gibsonburg, OH, in Ellen D. Dickinson, *New Light on Mormonism* (New York: Funk & Wagnalls, 1885), 260.

8. *The Susquehanna Register*, 1 May 1834.

9. Statement of E. D. Howe, 8 April 1885, Painesville, Lake

County, Ohio. Original in the Arthur Deming file, Mormon collection, Chicago Historical Society.

10. It is regrettable that Howe did not contact any of the Palmyra-Manchester witnesses, but his oversight is understandable considering the issues involved. The main target of the Mormon attack was the statement of Isaac Hale, which Howe had already authenticated, and the statements alleging that the Book of Mormon had been copied from a novel by Solomon Spaulding, which again Howe had verified.

11. Anderson, 286.

12. Chase had earlier repeated this charge in a statement made on 2 May 1879, Palmyra, Wayne County, NY; cited by William Wyl, *Mormon Portraits* . . . (Salt Lake City: Tribune Printing & Publishing Company, 1886), 230-31.

13. Howe, 262.

14. Tucker, 228-90. Unfortunately, Townsend did not say how much of his letter was based upon personal observation and how much upon hearsay, though it is unlikely that Townsend was merely reporting groundless rumors. His description of Martin Harris appears unusually accurate to anyone acquainted with the facts of Harris's life, and in at least one place he reveals information about Harris which was not generally known at the time. In discussing Smith's mysterious "gold plates," he quotes Harris's claim to have seen them with "spiritual eyes," a claim Harris repeated over the years to a number of people. Significantly, Townsend's letter, written in 1833 but not published until 1867, is the earliest of these reports.

15. Anderson, 291.

16. Statement of C. M. Stafford, 23 March 1885, Auburn, Ohio, cited by Arthur Deming, *Naked Truths About Mormonism* 2 (April 1888): 1.

17. Howe, 259, 260.

18. Tucker, 21.

19. Howe, 258. Among the "marvelous stories" Smith allegedly told Stafford was one in which he "showed me a piece of wood which he said he took from a box of money, and the

reason he gave for not obtaining the box, was that it *moved*." This story is significant because two of Smith's earliest and closest associates, Martin Harris and Orin Porter Rockwell, told a similar story years later in Utah. According to their independent reports, while digging for money in Palmyra, they uncovered a box of treasure. Anxious to secure the chest before it could slip back into the earth, one of their party struck the box with a pick, but the blow only succeeded in breaking off a piece of the lid. The treasure fled into the earth, leaving the diggers standing dumbfounded in the dark. Their only memento of the adventure was the piece of lid that had broken off the chest when struck. For these accounts, see Brigham Young et al., *Journal of Discourses*, 26 vols. (London: Latter-day Saints' Book Depot, 1855–86), 19:37, and the statement of Ole A. Jensen, July 1875, Clarkston, Utah, archives, historical department, Church of Jesus Christ of Latter-day Saints, Salt Lake City, Utah.

20. Anderson, 291.
21. Howe, 257.
22. See, for example, He. 12:18–19, 13:17–20, 32–37; Morm. 1:18–19; Eth. 14:1.
23. [Charles Marshall], "The Original Prophet," *Fraser's Magazine* 7 (Feb. 1873): 229–30. Although the authenticity of this trial record has been vigorously questioned, most historians now accept it as authentic. For a review of the matter, see Marvin S. Hill, "Joseph Smith and the 1826 Trial: New Evidence and New Difficulties," *Brigham Young University Studies* 12 (Winter 1972): 223–33.
24. Rejecting reported conversations as inadequate, Anderson is left only with observed actions upon which to base his assessment of Joseph Smith's early reputation. Such a principle, if conscientiously applied, may have a certain usefulness but as used by Anderson, its only purpose is to preempt the point. By stating at the outset what he shall accept as evidence and what not, Anderson not only eliminates the host of witnesses who claimed significant conversations with Smith but also creates a model of evidence which by defini-

tion cannot be satisfied. To prove involvement in money digging, he argues, the witness must actually have *seen* Smith
digging, and since "one might observe one of the Smiths
digging and completely misinterpret his reasons for doing
so" (p. 302), the witness must also have *heard* Smith say he
was digging for money. Since, however, reported conversations are "notoriously open to mistaken interpretation, recollection, and amplification" (p. 297), then it is possible that
Smith's words were "garbled" and thus are unacceptable as
evidence. In this manner Anderson constructs a model of evidence which guarantees the conclusion he is apparently seeking, namely that *no* report, however well authenticated, can
prove that Smith was a money digger.

25. Howe, 249.
26. Anderson, 292. The quotation Anderson makes is from Joseph
    Smith's journal as kept by Willard Richards, entry for 1 Jan-
    uary 1843, in Scott H. Faulring, ed., *An American Prophet's
    Record: The Diaries and Journals of Joseph Smith* (Salt Lake City:
    Signature Books and Smith Research Associates, 1987), 267.
27. The fact that Smith only imperfectly remembered Stafford's
    affidavit is found in his remark that the seven men who at-
    tacked him were the ones who signed the statement, whereas
    in fact Stafford was alone in making the deposition.
28. Anderson, 292.
29. Smith was married on 18 January 1827.
30. Anderson, 293.

Chapter 4

THE HURLBUT AFFIDAVITS

PART TWO

ichard Anderson's treatment of Philastus Hurlbut's longer affidavits follows a pattern similar to his approach to the shorter ones. He rejects Willard Chase's testimony because of Chase's "nearly total lack of personal observation" and because Chase himself was a money digger. He rejects William Stafford's affidavit because he finds Stafford's "black sheep" story dubious. Anderson suggests that Hurlbut wrote the statement and merely had Stafford sign it. Anderson then dismisses Peter Ingersoll's testimony because it mainly "consists not in observation, but supposed admissions in conversation" and because Anderson finds reason to doubt one of those reported confessions.[1] Of these criticisms, some are based on entirely erroneous information and some reflect partial truth and partial error. But none justify Anderson's conclusion that the affidavits are essentially "non-evidence."

Anderson claims that of the three longer affidavits, Willard Chase's is probably the most authentic. He finds less Hurlbut in the Chase affidavit and observes that "the Chase statement contains more parallels to Mormon sources." Chase was probably more careful in making his deposition, Anderson suggests, because of his standing in the Methodist church. But despite these strengths, Anderson still considers Chase essentially a non-witness. According to Anderson, Chase's information was hearsay. Chase tells the "familiar story" of finding an unusual stone while digging a well with Alvin and Joseph Smith, and accuses Joseph and Hyrum of duplicity in keeping the object. Beyond that, according to Anderson, he discloses no direct knowledge that the stone was utilized in treasure digging, but only alleges that Joseph claimed to discover "wonders" by its use.[2]

A number of points should be made concerning this statement. First, the so-called "familiar story" recounted by Chase is familiar only because it is so well authenticated. Chase was in the well at the time the stone was discovered, and it was he, not Smith, who brought it to the surface in order to examine it more closely. According to Chase, "Joseph put it into his hat, and then his face into the top of his hat. . . . The next morning he came to me, and wished to obtain the stone, alledging that he could see in it; but I told him I did not wish to part with it on account of its being a curiosity, but would lend it. After obtaining the stone, he began to publish abroad what wonders he could discover by looking in it, and made so much disturbance among the credulous part of [the] community, that I ordered the stone to be returned to me again."[3] Chase, as Anderson observes, does not say explicitly what "wonders" Smith saw in the stone, but other witnesses have not been so reserved. Joseph Smith himself acknowledged in 1826 that he used the stone "to determine where hidden treasures in the bowels of the earth were," and Smith's mother recorded that her son had in his possession a marvelous instrument "by which he could discern things invisible to the naked eye" and that it was this which led Josiah Stowell to hire him as a money digger in 1825.[4] Many other witnesses mention Smith's stone and the "ghosts, infernal spirits, mountains of gold and silver" which he claimed to see within its depths.[5]

Anderson briefly mentions, but without comment, Chase's accusation that Smith and his brother Hyrum were guilty of duplicity in keeping the stone without Chase's permission. Chase asserts as a matter of personal observation that Smith borrowed the stone from him in 1822, returned it about two years later, and borrowed it again in 1825. In 1826 Chase asked Smith for the stone and was refused and in 1830 was refused again by Hyrum Smith, who would not return the object because "Joseph made use of it in translating his Bible." When Chase reminded Smith of his promise to return the rock, Smith called him a liar and "in a rage shook his fist at me, and abused me in a most scandalous manner."[6] Since Joseph Smith acknowledged to others that the stone was borrowed,[7] and since he never returned it to Chase despite repeated requests, the conclusion seems justified that, at least on this occasion, Smith retained possession of an object that was not lawfully his.

Anderson finds it necessary to discredit Chase's description of Smith as a money digger by arguing that Chase claimed no firsthand knowledge of the fact and that since Chase was a money digger himself, "the conclusion follows that the Smiths did not have a connection with the money digging circles in the area."[8] Anderson's conclusion would follow only if the various money-digging circles operating in the area were acting in concert, but all available evidence suggests that they were competitive rather than cooperative. Many contemporaries remarked on the secrecy which attended money-digging operations. The reason for this is not difficult to guess. A person who believes that he will shortly uncover a treasure of tremendous value is not likely to tell too many others, fearing they will find it first. The trouble Joseph Smith had with other money diggers after he was said to have unearthed gold plates illustrates perfectly why each band of diggers was secretive in its operations, rarely consulting each other unless it was to their mutual advantage. Much of Smith's attention for the next few years was devoted to concealing the location of the unearthed plates. Under such conditions it would be unlikely that Chase, whose sister was a seeress, would ever observe the operations of Smith's company, although he would probably have heard of them indirectly.[9]

Anderson dismisses Chase's secondhand descriptions of Smith's money digging in Pennsylvania as "highly distorted" because Chase's descriptions of known events in Smith's life differ from later, Mormon sources. He lists as a typical example Chase's "exaggerated, ridiculing details" about Smith's first failure to obtain the plates.[10] Anderson assumes what must first be proved, namely that other, later accounts are more accurate because they lack the "exaggerated" details remembered by Chase. It is equally reasonable to assume, however, that Smith himself later deleted such details so as to give no support to those who charged that his story of finding the gold plates was just another adaptation of the old money-digging theme.

To a considerable degree this can be shown to be the case. Smith's official report of his first visit to the Hill Cumorah is spartan when compared with the more richly detailed accounts preserved by those who heard the story from Smith or his father before 1830. The descriptions of Smith's mother, Oliver Cowdery, Joseph Knight, Hiel and Joseph Lewis, Lorenzo Saunders, and Fayette Lapham confirm to an impressive degree the details remembered by Chase, including such specifics as Joseph Smith being struck or shocked when he attempted to touch the plates; the vanishing of the plates when Smith laid them on the ground and their sudden reappearance in the buried box from which he had taken them; the exchange between Smith and the guardian spirit as to why the plates could not then be obtained; the spirit's instructions to bring his eldest brother, Alvin, with him next time and Alvin's premature death; and finally the spirit's commandment to bring another person whom Smith would recognize on sight and who later turned out to be Emma Hale.

It is not difficult to guess why such "details" might reasonably be omitted from Smith's official history many years later. It was illegal at the time to pretend "to tell fortunes, or to discover where lost good may be found."[11] Joseph Knight's recollection that Smith "looked in his glass"[12] to find the right person to bring with him to the hill would elicit memories of the glass-looking charge Joseph Smith was convicted of in 1826. Smith was learning from bitter experience that not everyone shared his enthusiasm for the supernatural.

If there is no ground for Anderson's claim that Chase's account of Smith's visit to the Hill Cumorah is riddled with "exaggerated, ridiculing details," then his assertion that "one would assume the same of his secondhand treasure stories" simply does not follow.[13] Indeed, the man Chase named as his source for these details told the same account to Lorenzo Saunders. According to Saunders, "Sam Lawrence took him [Smith] over into Pennsylvania and introduced him to Emma Hale. I dont know as Joe had ever been in Pennsylvania before, but him and Sam Lawrence had been deviling around—no telling where they had gone. Joe told Sam Lawrence that there was a silver mine over in Pennsylvania told him he might share in it with him; but behold he wanted an introduction to Emma Hale is the way it turned out. Sam Lawrence told me so."[14] This is virtually the same story recounted by Chase "as related to me by Lawrence himself," which seems to verify the essential accuracy of Chase's memory.[15] Following Anderson's reasoning, "one would assume the same" of his entire report.

The next deposition Anderson considers is that of William Stafford. Anderson's first charge is that Hurlbut probably wrote Stafford's affidavit and "merely had him sign it,"[16] which even if true does not mean that Stafford's statement is not a genuine reflection of his views. When he appeared before Judge Baldwin "and made oath to the truth of the above statement, and signed the same," he legally and morally became responsible for its contents, which hardly justifies Anderson's "merely." There is, however, no real evidence that Hurlbut wrote Stafford's affidavit. Anderson's only reason is that "Pomeroy Tucker portrays Stafford as a former sailor without education."[17] But Tucker says nothing about Stafford's education, only that he "had been for many years a sailor, and was largely prone to the vagaries and superstitions peculiar to his class."[18] Tucker's comment may reveal something about Stafford's "will to believe," but it says nothing about whether he was capable of writing an affidavit.

Anderson seems uncomfortable to find in Stafford's deposition an eyewitness account by someone participating with the Smiths in a treasure hunt. The extent of Anderson's discomfort is clear from the lengths he goes to discredit Stafford, for nowhere else does he commit so many mistakes in so little space. If he cannot discredit Stafford, then he is left with a witness who actually participated with the Smiths in one dig, offered them support in another, and recounted at length "the marvellous tales" they told him "respecting the discoveries they had made in the peculiar occupation of money digging."[19] Stafford's testimony, if allowed to pass unchallenged, would also lend an air of credence to reports offered by Hurlbut's other witnesses; and since Anderson's purpose is to prove Hurlbut's witnesses incompetent, he is anxious to avoid any statement which might reflect favorably on their collective testimony. It seems easier for Anderson to disagree with the collective neighborhood interpretation of these events than with the basic information supplied by the neighbors about what happened, when, and who was involved.

Nevertheless, Anderson mentions Stafford's "one clear firsthand testimony" only to dismiss it because "the accompanying sheep story throws a great deal of doubt on the digging story as authentically coming from Stafford."[20] That story, as related by Stafford, is as follows: "At another time, they devised a scheme, by which they might satiate their hunger, with the mutton of one of my sheep. They had seen in my flock of sheep, a large, fat, black weather. Old Joseph and one of the boys came to me one day, and said that Joseph Jr. had discovered some very remarkable and valuable treasures, which could be procured only in one way. That way, was as follows:—That a black sheep should be taken on the ground where the treasures were concealed—that after cutting its throat, it should be led around a circle while bleeding. This being done, the wrath of the evil spirit would be appeased: the treasures could then be obtained, and my share of them was to be four fold. To gratify my curiosity, I let them have a large fat sheep. They afterwards informed me, that the sheep was killed pursuant to commandment; but as there was some mistake in the process, it did not have the desired effect. This, I believe, is the only time they ever made money-digging a profitable business."[21]

Anderson argues that "Hurlbut evidently did not represent Stafford accurately." His stated reason is that Wallace Miner, who was born in 1843, one year before Smith died, related in the early 1930s a story Stafford told him some time before Stafford's death on 9 January 1863. According to Miner, Stafford told him that Smith took the sheep without Stafford's knowledge but the next day confessed the theft and offered to make restitution by making wooden sap buckets until the sheep was paid for. Anderson admits the "obvious limitations in recalling the details of what one had said almost seventy years earlier" about an event that occurred forty years before that, but he accepts the story because it "exonerates the Smiths of dishonesty, a reversal of Hurlbut reporting Stafford."[22]

This appeal to Miner's story is perhaps the most egregious of Anderson's errors. The difficulty with Anderson's witness cannot be avoided by candidly admitting his "obvious limitations" and then proceeding as if they did not exist. In addition, by accepting Miner's testimony Anderson is forced to abandon one of his own most important criteria for competent reporting. If, as Anderson argues, the fallibility of human memory makes remembered conversations such as those collected by Hurlbut unreliable, how can he accept Miner's report? Hurlbut collected his statements mostly from people who were remembering events which occurred on the average less than a decade earlier, whereas Miner was remembering a conversation that had taken place nearly two generations before.

Anderson's approach to this particular story demonstrates an additional inadequacy: the problem of how he can consider Miner's report "a reversal of Hurlbut reporting Stafford" when the statement collected by Hurlbut does not accuse Smith of stealing the sheep. Stafford says he "let them *have* a large fat sheep" as his investment in the digging enterprise. Stafford does allude vaguely to sheep stealing on the part of Smith's associates,[23] but nowhere does he accuse the family of taking the animal without his consent.[24]

Although Anderson wants to prove that Hurlbut "contaminated" Stafford's report since Miner's report of Stafford differs from Hurlbut's report of Stafford, the evidence he adduces proves exactly the opposite. As has been shown,

Miner's report, which depicts Smith as a thief stricken by a conscience, confirms rather than denies the allegation of dishonesty on the part of the Smiths. Hurlbut's reporting of Stafford, on the other hand, pointedly states that there was nothing dishonest in the means used by the Smiths to procure the sheep. This is odd if Hurlbut's purpose was to impugn the honesty of the Smiths, for why should Hurlbut have Stafford state that he let them have a sheep when Stafford actually accused them of stealing the animal? For Hurlbut to exonerate the Smiths and then imply their guilt by means of a veiled allusion to the habits of their companions is incomprehensible if Stafford in fact told Hurlbut what he allegedly told Miner, which if true would mean that the relentlessly vindictive Hurlbut had exercised his "evident editorializing talents" not to accuse the Smiths but to defend them. From this it is apparent that Anderson's conclusion—"Miner's recollection of Stafford exonerates the Smiths of dishonesty, a reversal of Hurlbut reporting Stafford"—needs itself to be reversed.

The attempt to prove that Hurlbut adversely influenced Stafford's report is further discredited by comparing that account with other recollections of the sheep story which evidently do not depend on Hurlbut's version. When Stephen S. Harding was visiting friends in Palmyra during the summer of 1829, he heard the same story Stafford would relate to Hurlbut in 1833 and corroborated Pomeroy Tucker's version of the event as essentially the same story circulating in Palmyra over four years before Hurlbut ever visited the area.[25] Tucker's version is also in harmony with William Stafford's account.[26] The Miner report, if trustworthy at all, provides additional information, agreeing with the preceding statements, that the sheep was used as a sacrifice to secure buried treasure and that Smith traced "a circle within which the wether was placed and his throat cut; the blood saturated the ground."[27] There is thus evidence that the story Stafford told Hurlbut in 1833 corresponded in nearly every particular with what he was saying both before and after that date, a conclusion hardly compatible with Anderson's claim that Hurlbut twisted Stafford's statement to make it appear worse than it actually was.[28]

Anderson's final reason for doubting Stafford's story is a reported conversation with Dr. John Stafford, who supposedly told the Kelleys in 1881, "I have heard that story, but don't think my father was there at the time they say Smith got the sheep. I don't know anything about it."[29] Despite Stafford's "I don't know anything about it," he reportedly told the Kelleys, "I don't think it is true. I would have heard more about it. That is true." If the Kelleys are here accurately reporting Stafford's words, he is simply confessing his ignorance of the event. "I don't know anything about it," he says. "I don't think it is true." This confession adds nothing to the question of the accuracy of his father William's deposition. His "I don't think it is true" is a conclusion based upon ignorance, not upon any facts which came under his observation.[30]

Still, it would be odd if William Stafford's son should suspect the truthfulness of a story repeated so often by his father and sworn to before a judge if he did not have good reason for his opinion. It remains to be determined, however, if John Stafford harbored any of the doubts about the story attributed to him by the Kelleys. One ground for suspicion is that the Kelleys' published report was challenged by some of their interviewees only days after it first appeared, the Kelleys being charged with gross and willful falsification in putting words into their witnesses' mouths. Another cause for suspicion is that the notes from which William Kelley reconstructed these interviews contain nothing suggesting that John Stafford was less than confident about the story told by his father. According to those notes, all Stafford said about the incident was "My father is said to have furnished a sheep—but I don't think my father was there at [the] time they say [the] sheep was sacrificed."[31] In preparing this material for publication, William Kelley replaced the word "sacrificed" with "got the sheep," and then added a lengthy question-and-answer section in which Stafford not only confessed his ignorance of the matter but also expressed suspicion that the whole story is a fabrication. Deleting this added material, Stafford's report to the Kelleys contains only the information that he had heard the story but did not think his father was there at the time of the sheep's sacrifice. This agrees perfectly with his father's recollection that he was not present when the sheep was "killed pursuant to commandment."[32]

If, as I have suggested, there is no good reason for doubting Stafford's story of the slaughtered sheep, then Anderson's argument that the episode can be used to cast suspicion on the integrity of other parts of Stafford's report can be dismissed. As an authentic recollection, the sheep story not only adds to the evidence that Smith hunted for treasure by magical means but also lends support to that part of Stafford's affidavit in which Stafford describes himself as actually joining the Smiths in a dig. Stafford recounts that story as follows: "Joseph Smith, Sen., came to me one night, and told me, that Joseph Jr. had been looking in his glass, and had seen, not many rods from his house, two or three kegs of gold and silver, some feet under the surface of the earth; and that none others but the elder Joseph and myself could get them. I accordingly consented to go, and early in the evening repaired to the place of deposit. Joseph, Sen. first made a circle, twelve or fourteen feet in diameter. This circle, said he, contains the treasure. He then stuck in the ground a row of witch hazel sticks, around the said circle, for the purpose of keeping off the evil spirits. Within this circle he made another, of about eight or ten feet in diameter. He walked around three times on the periphery of this last circle, muttering to himself something which I could not understand. He next stuck a steel rod in the centre of the circles, and then enjoined profound silence upon us, lest we should arouse the evil spirit who had the charge of these treasures. After we had dug a trench about five feet in depth around the rod, the old man by signs and motions, asked leave of absence, and went to the house to inquire of young Joseph the cause of our disappointment. He soon returned and said, that Joseph had remained all this time in the house, looking in his stone and watching the motions of the evil spirit—that he saw the spirit come up to the ring and as soon as it beheld the cone which we had formed around the rod, it caused the money to sink. We then went into the house, and the old man observed, that we had made a mistake in the commencement of the operation; if it had not been for that, said he, we should have got the money."[33]

The evidential strength of this recollection can best be appreciated by considering how inappropriate Anderson's standard counter-explanations become when applied to it. For example, Anderson's suggestion that the plethora of money-digging stories about the Smiths can be attributed to an "erroneous parallel" between the Mormon Smiths and another Smith family whose members were actually money diggers is untenable in light of the testimony of a witness like William Stafford, who lived next to the Smiths for more than a decade and who knew them both as money diggers and as founders of a church. Equally inapplicable is the suggestion that Stafford may have witnessed Joseph Smith, Sr., engaged in some legitimate digging project and misinterpreted the action because of rumors describing the activities of local money diggers. Stafford was not a casual observer but an active participant in the dig; he was specifically told that the digging was for treasure and witnessed the magical rituals used by the elder

Smith to immobilize the treasure and ward off evil spirits. Finally, there is no evidence that the Smiths were employees of someone else in this venture. It was they who took the initiative to invite Stafford, not he them, and the only evidence of a "boss" of the operation is Joseph Smith, who supervised from the house, "looking in his stone and watching the motions of the evil spirit." Stafford's affidavit thus provides an effective refutation of Anderson's contention, "There is no solid evidence of Joseph Smith as the prime mover in any treasure seeking project."[34]

The last of the Hurlbut affidavits Anderson considers is that of Peter Ingersoll. In his deposition, Ingersoll rehearses various efforts of the elder Smith to make him a money digger, recalls conversations with him about divination and money digging, and relates an episode in which Joseph Smith, Sr., found some lost cows by means of a witch hazel stick. Ingersoll dismisses this later accomplishment as a trick to test his credulity. Ingersoll tells of being hired by Joseph Smith, Jr., to go with him to Pennsylvania to help move Smith's new wife Emma's furniture back to Manchester, describes an episode along the way in which Smith supposedly displayed some Yankee ingenuity to avoid paying a toll, repeats an alleged confession that the business of the gold plates was nothing more than a ruse to deceive his parents, recounts Smith's successful effort to get fifty dollars from Martin Harris, and narrates a number of other episodes said to have been drawn from his personal knowledge of the Smith family.

Anderson's analysis of Ingersoll's deposition is limited to the confession that the gold plates were a hoax. According to Ingersoll, Smith told him that he had discovered some white sand that had been washed out after a storm. Impressed with the beauty and purity of the sand, Smith tied several quarts of it up in his farmer's smock and carried it home. His response when his parents expressed curiosity about what he had in his smock, according to Ingersoll, was: " '[I] happened to think of what I had heard about a history found in Canada, called the golden Bible; so I very gravely told them it was the golden Bible. To my surprise, they were credulous enough to believe what I said. Accordingly I told them that I had received a commandment to let no one see it, for, says I, no man can see it with the naked eye and live. However, I offered to take out the book and show it to them, but they refused to see it, and left the room.' Now, said Jo, 'I have got the damned fools fixed, and will carry out the fun.' "[35]

Of all the information volunteered by Hurlbut's witness, Ingersoll's story is the most dubious for a number of reasons. First, Ingersoll represents the incident as unpremeditated deception on Smith's part. Aside from all other considerations, there exists ample evidence that Smith had been talking about the gold plates some time before the date Ingersoll attaches to this prank. Second, Smith's known regard for his parents makes it unlikely that he would deceive them for the sheer fun of it, call them "damned fools" and perpetrate the hoax for the rest of his life. Third, Ingersoll records that after this confession of duplicity he offered to loan Smith sufficient money to move to Pennsylvania, which is unlikely if Smith was in fact the knave Ingersoll knew him to be. Last—and perhaps the most significant consideration—Pomeroy Tucker remembered that Ingersoll "was at first inclined to put faith in his [Smith's] 'Golden Bible' pretension."[36] If Tucker's statement can be trusted, it seems likely that Ingersoll created the story as a way of striking back at Smith for his own gullibility in swallowing a story he later became convinced was a hoax.

The "white sand" story casts a shadow of suspicion over Ingersoll's entire affidavit, but it does not follow that every part of his statement is false. For instance, according to Ingersoll Smith promised Isaac Hale "to give up his old habits of digging for money and looking into stones" and gratefully accepted Hale's offer of financial support if Smith "would move to Pennsylvania and work for a living." According to Hale's independent account of the same conversation, "Smith stated to me, that he had given up what he called 'glass-looking,' and that he expected to work hard for a living, and was willing to do so," and Hale's son Alva remembered Smith as saying "that he intended to quit the business, (of peeping) and labor for his livelihood." Ingersoll also stated that on this same occasion, Smith "acknowledged he could not see in a stone now, nor ever could." This was remembered by Alva Hale, who quoted Smith as saying "that this *'peeping'* was all d − −d nonsense. He (Smith) was deceived himself but did not intend to deceive others."[37] These parallels do not substantiate Ingersoll's "white sand" story, but they confirm that Smith publicly acknowledged his career as a "glass looker" and money digger.

Anderson asserts that Hurlbut purposely avoided collecting any information that would have been positive. "Obviously, the attempt was made only to discredit − not to gather authentic information. Because history is the art of seeing both sides of the balance sheet, Hurlbut produced mere propaganda."[38] Granting that Hurlbut was not impartial does not mean that an investigator less biased would have produced significantly different results.[39] For example, when newspaper reporter James Gordon Bennett visited western New York in 1831 to find out the truth about Joseph Smith and the famous "gold Bible," he was told that Smith was "a careless, indolent, idle, and shiftless" money digger and that the whole Smith family were "readier at inventing stories and tales than attending church or engaging in any industrious trade."[40] Similarly, when John S. Carter, a Mormon, visited the area in 1833, he found "The people greatly opposed to the work of God. Talked with many of them & found them unable to make out anything against Joseph Smith, altho they talked hard against him."[41] The only real difference between Carter's and Hurlbut's experience was that the latter was apparently more successful in finding witnesses who could provide reasons for their opinion of Joseph Smith.

NOTES

1. Richard L. Anderson, "Joseph Smith's New York Reputation Reappraised," *Brigham Young University Studies* 10 (Spring 1970): 296, 293, 298.
2. Ibid., 296.
3. Eber D. Howe, *Mormonism Unvailed* . . . (Painesville, OH: Printed and published by the author, 1834), 241.
4. [Charles Marshall], "The Original Prophet," *Fraser's Magazine* 7 (Feb. 1873): 229; Lucy Mack Smith, *Biographical Sketches* . . . (Liverpool: S. W. Richards, 1853), 92.
5. Howe, 259; compare pp. 237–38.
6. Ibid., 247.
7. See, for example, W. R. Hine's statement in Arthur B. Deming, *Naked Truths About Mormonism* 1 (Jan. 1888): 2.
8. Anderson, 297.
9. Chase's sources of information could have been his sister Sallie and Samuel Lawrence. After Smith returned the stone in 1824 and before he borrowed it again in 1825, he would ask Sallie to consult the stone regarding the best place to search for buried treasures (so Sallie told Mrs. S. F. Anderick. See her statement in Deming 1:2). Samuel T. Lawrence, a local farmer whom Chase names as the source for his description of Smith's gold hunting in Pennsylvania, was one of Smith's regular supporters until some time after Smith announced the existence of the gold plates. Apparently the two men were once quite intimate, for according to Chase it was Lawrence whom Smith first showed the spot where the plates were deposited. Later Smith claimed that he had not shown Lawrence the right place because, in the words of early Mormon

Joseph Knight, Lawrence "was a Seear and he had Bin to the hill and knew the things in the hill and was trying to obtain them." Dean Jessee, "Joseph Knight's Recollection of Early Mormon History," *Brigham Young University Studies* 17 (Autumn 1976): 32. Later Lawrence joined Willard and Sallie Chase in their efforts to locate Smith's elusive treasure.

10. Anderson, 297.
11. *Laws of the State of New York, Revised and Passed . . .* 2 vols. (1813), 1:114, in Wesley P. Walters, "From Occult to Cult with Joseph Smith, Jr.," *The Journal of Pastoral Practice* 1 (Summer 1977): 124.
12. Jessee, 31.
13. Anderson, 297.
14. Statement of Lorenzo Saunders, 17 Sept. 1884, Reading, MI, 11, archives, Reorganized Church of Jesus Christ of Latter Day Saints, Independence, Missouri.
15. Howe, 243.
16. Anderson, 293.
17. Ibid.
18. Pomeroy Tucker, *The Origin, Rise and Progress of Mormonism* (New York: D. Appleton and Co., 1867), 24.
19. Howe, 237.
20. Anderson, 294.
21. Howe, 239.
22. Anderson, 294.
23. Howe, 239.
24. If Anderson were genuinely interested in answering the charge of sheep stealing, a more worthy candidate is David Stafford. According to him, "At different times I have seen them [the Smiths] come from the woods early in the morning, bringing meat which looked like mutton. I went into the woods one morning very early, shooting patridges and found Joseph Smith Sen. in company with two other men, with hoes, shovels and meat that looked like mutton. On seeing me they run like wild men to get out of sight—Seeing the old man a few day afterwards, I asked him why he run so the other day in the woods, ah said he, you know that circumstances alter

cases; it will not do to be seen at all time" (Howe, 249–50). Anderson, however, does not attempt to answer this accusation, preferring instead to make the charge rest upon nothing more substantial than "intended implication."

25. Letter of Stephen S. Harding to Thomas Gregg, February 1882, Milan, IN, in Thomas Gregg, *The Prophet of Palmyra* . . . (New York: John B. Alden, Publisher, 1890), 56; compare Tucker, 24–25.

26. Deming 1:3. Anderson dismisses Cornelius Stafford's retelling of the story as "exaggerated." However, the only difference between the two versions is that William recorded that Smith led the sheep "around a circle while bleeding" while Cornelius recorded that Smith led the sheep around the circle three times. Since William did not state how many times the sheep made the circuit, only that it did so "while bleeding," there exists no reason to accuse Cornelius of exaggerating even on this point.

27. Thomas L. Cook, *Palmyra and Vicinity* (Palmyra, NY: Press of the Palmyra Courier-Journal, 1930), 222. For still another recollection of the sheep story, see Andrew Jenson and Edward Stevenson, *Infancy of the Church* . . . (Salt Lake City: n.p., 1889), 40–41.

28. Anderson might respond that the witnesses all composed their statements years after the publication of Hurlbut's affidavits and that reading Stafford's report "contaminated" their memories. Harding's lengthy letter, however, displays no sign of familiarity with Hurlbut's statements. Neither is it certain that Tucker used them in writing his own book. In fact, the disparities between some of Hurlbut's depositions and parts of Tucker's book make it unlikely that he was using the affidavits at all. Tucker probably depended instead for his information upon his own memory and the verbal testimony of still living witnesses. Despite this, Anderson claims that "Tucker depicted superstitious and unscrupulous Smiths by merely requoting the 1833 statements" (p. 304).

29. William K. Kelley, "The Hill Cumorah . . . The Stories of

Hurlbert, Howe, Tucker, &c. from Late Interviews," *Saints'
Herald* 28 (1 June 1881): 167; hereafter Kelley, "Interviews."

30. As Anderson reminds us, "The rules of evidence in the United
States insist that a witness tell specific experiences, and leave
to the court or jury the function of forming opinions from
them" (p. 290).

31. William H. Kelley notebook, "Interviews and accounts," 19–20,
RLDS church archives; hereafter Kelley, "Notes."

32. In his debate with E. L. Kelley in 1884, Clark Braden claimed
that Stafford never told Kelley "his own father's affidavit in
regard to the black wether was false. I will furnish Dr.
Stafford's affidavit that it is true." I have been unable to determine if Braden carried out his promise, but in view of
Kelley's own notes and the published interview based upon
them, it does appear unlikely that Stafford denied the story
as Kelley claimed he did. For Braden's statement, see E. L.
Kelley and Clark Braden, *Public Discussion of the Issues Between
the Reorganized Church of Jesus Christ of Latter Day Saints and
the Church of Christ (Disciples)* . . . (St. Louis: Christian Publishing Co., 1884), 370–71.

33. Howe, 238–39.

34. Anderson, 303–304.

35. Howe, 236.

36. Tucker, 128; compare pp. 38–39.

37. Howe, 234–35, 264, 268. Other parts of Ingersoll's affidavit
can also be independently confirmed. His claim that he was
hired by Smith to go to Pennsylvania and move Emma's furniture back to Manchester was confirmed by Isaac Hale; his
account of Smith's unsuccessful attempt to get Willard Chase
to make a box for the gold plates was confirmed by Chase;
and his report that Smith approached Martin Harris with the
remark, "I had a command to ask the first *honest man* I met
with, for fifty dollars in money, and he would let me have it"
was confirmed by both Chase and Jesse Townsend. More
significant than these confirmations, however, is his claim
that Joseph Smith, Sr., possessed a magical rod. This is significant not only because many others mention the elder

Smith's rod but also because it can now be shown that the report by no means originated with Ingersoll or even the vitriolic editorials of Abner Cole in 1831. On 17 June 1829, Jesse Smith, the brother of Joseph Smith, Sr., wrote a letter to Hyrum Smith in which he mentions a messenger sent by the elder Smith to tell his relatives of young Joseph's wonderful "gold book." This messenger "believes all to be a fact. . . . [H]e says your father has a wand or rod can tell the distance from India to Ethiopia. . . . " (copy in archives, historical department, Church of Jesus Christ of Latter-day Saints, Salt Lake City, Utah).

38. Anderson, 299.

39. John A. Clark's comment is typical of many others: "There are no Mormons in Manchester, or Palmyra, the place where this Book of Mormon was pretended to be found. You might as well go down into the Crater of Vesuvius and attempt to build an ice house amid its molten and boiling lava, as to convince any inhabitant of either of these towns, that Jo Smith's pretensions are not the most gross and egregious falsehood. It was indeed a wise stroke of policy, for those who got up this imposture, and who calculated to make their fortune by it, to emigrate to a place where they were wholly unknown." *Gleanings by the Way* (Philadelphia: W. J. & J. K. Simon, 1842), 346.

40. New York *Morning Courier and Enquirer*, 31 Aug. 1831, in Leonard J. Arrington, "James Gordon Bennett's 1831 Report on 'The Mormonites,' " *Brigham Young University Studies* 10 (Spring 1970): 357–58.

41. Diary of John S. Carter, in Davis Bitton, *Guide to Mormon Diaries and Autobiographies* (Provo, UT: Brigham Young University Press, 1977), 62.

Chapter 5

THE DEMING AFFIDAVITS

ext in his reappraisal of Joseph Smith's New York reputation, Richard Anderson describes the depositions collected by Arthur B. Deming in the mid-1880s as "biased" and "one-sided." Anderson accuses Deming of "Hurlbut-like prompting or editing" and dismisses Deming's firsthand reports of Joseph Smith's drinking and fighting because their language is "standard enough to have come from a common compiler." He alleges that the reports contain no actual observation of Smith's money digging. Deming himself Anderson characterizes as "neurotically resentful" and "a pathetic reincarnation of the disgruntled Hurlbut."[1]

Of these various charges, most simply lack serious thought. Among Deming's informants was one who described Smith's mother Lucy Mack as a kind old woman who "doctored many persons in Palmyra" and another who described Smith's younger brother Samuel as "a good, industrious boy."[2] Obviously these are not "one-sided reports from biased people," nor do they lend credence to Anderson's claim that Deming used Hurlbut-like tactics in collecting his depositions. According to Anderson, Hurlbut's methods of gathering information resulted in the "unmodified condemnation of Joseph Smith and his entire family," yet Anderson admits that Deming "does not totally damn the Smiths as Hurlbut-Howe."[3] Deming is thus condemned because he displays Hurlbut-like qualities which Anderson admits are not really Hurlbut-like at all.

Actually, few early writers on Mormonism are less deserving of the epithet "Hurlbut-like" than Deming. There exists no evidence that Deming adversely influenced his witnesses, edited their recollections, or contacted only those unfriendly to the Smiths. Not only do the depositions themselves belie such charges, but evidence exists suggesting that Deming was aware of such possible objections and had taken precautions against them. Having acted as moderator and research consultant for Clark Braden during the latter's famous debate with E. L. Kelley in 1884, Deming was more than aware of the Kelleys continuing efforts to discredit all unfavorable testimony about the character of Joseph Smith. He had not long been engaged in the work of collecting affidavits about Smith when he discovered that the Kelleys had interviewed at least one of his witnesses before him.[4] Deming consequently tried whenever possible to have the affidavits attested to by more than just the interviewee. Most were notarized, witnessed by friends or relatives present at the time, and printed complete with addresses of the original testators.[5] In this manner Deming not only guaranteed the authenticity of the statements but also provided potential critics with the information necessary to discredit him if they suspected that any of the statements were false.

In Deming's case, a few supporting documents have survived which better enable one to evaluate his competence as an historian. In the Chicago Historical Society are the original of one published deposition and other statements which Deming had no opportunity to publish.[6] None support Anderson's allegation that Deming led his witnesses or improperly edited their remarks. The original statement of K. E. Bell, published in the first issue of Deming's newspaper, seems to be in Bell's own hand and is signed by the author, witnessed by another person, and notarized by a justice of the peace. It does not differ significantly from the printed version. In other statements Deming apparently acted as an amanuensis for his witnesses, but even in these instances I can find no evidence that he recorded more (or less) than his testators remembered. The statement of Eber D. Howe, for example, is signed by Howe, witnessed by Deming and a grandson, and concludes: "This statement was read in presence of Mr. Howe his daughter and grand son before being signed."[7] Also among this collection is the unpublished statement of J. C. Dowen, which similarly concludes: "I have heard Mr. Deming read this statement distinctly and make it as the last important act of my li[fe]." The statement was then witnessed by a granddaughter and grandson, notarized by a justice of the peace, and concluded with a note from that same justice: "At J. C. Dowen's request I was present and heard A. B. Deming read distinctly this statement to Mr. Dowen before being signed, which he said was correct."[8]

After studied analysis, Deming's report must stand as one of the most careful, conscientious, and energetic efforts to gather information about Joseph Smith from still living witnesses. Deming's methods would not be considered satisfactory today, but they were for the time above the norm and reveal a determination on his part to escape the sorts of criticisms leveled against Hurlbut. The effort cost Deming heavily in time and money, and he later came to deeply regret the "nearly four years hard labor, self-denial, and persecutions" he underwent while completing the project.[9] Deming's primary deficiency was that he had to depend upon witnesses separated from the events they were narrating by sixty or more years. This is one reason why Deming should be read in conjunction with Hurlbut, whose witnesses, however hostile, were removed by only a few years from actual contact with the Smith family.

Deming's depositions, together with the statements collected by Hurlbut, are important for two reasons. First, they reveal that some of Hurlbut's witnesses were less than candid about their own relationship with the Smiths. For example, when Willard Chase wrote his affidavit in 1833, he did not bother explaining his interest in the "singularly appearing stone" dug from his well, only that it "excited my curiosity." Deming's witnesses, however, describe Chase himself as a money digger and his sister as a seeress. If true, such facts would explain Chase's initial interest in the stone and his repeated efforts to get it back. Neither does Joshua Stafford in the statement he prepared for Hurlbut admit that he was himself once a money digger who dug with "the infamous Joe Smith." Smith's notoriety as a money digger may have made both men reluctant to admit publicly their own faith in seer stones and buried treasures.

If Deming's statements reveal something of what Hurlbut's witnesses chose not to divulge about themselves, they at the same time lend additional credence to some of Hurlbut's statements. The Chase stone episode, Stafford's black sheep story, and Barton Stafford's testimony that Smith got drunk while haying for Stafford's father, William, were described by S. F. Anderick and Christopher and Cornelius Stafford. Besides such direct confirmations, Deming's witnesses also provided additional statements about drinking and money digging. "I have frequently seen old Jo drunk," Isaac Butts recorded. Cornelius R. Stafford remembered seeing "Jo in drunken fights; father and son were frequently drunk." And Christopher M. Stafford testified: "Jo got drunk while we were haying for my uncle, Wm. Stafford; also at a husking at our house, and stayed overnight. I have often seen him drunk."

On the matter of money digging, many described the divining rod and seer stone and told of their use by Smith in locating buried treasures. Conversations about money digging are recounted, and at least two people claimed to have seen Smith hunting for "lost and hidden things" while in Pennsylvania. Wrote Henry A. Sayer, "I became acquainted with Jo, Hyrum, and Bill [William, a younger brother] Smith, whom I often saw hunting and digging for buried money, treasure, or lost and hidden things." W. R. Hine remembered seeing Joseph Smith hunting salt with his seer stone for at least two summers. Not only did this occur "near and in sight of my house," but when it rained Hine and his wife "made beds for them on the floor in our house."[10]

Anderson wants to ascribe to Deming the accounts of Smith's drinking and fighting, but he concentrates on what he sees as authentic statements implicating the Chases and Staffords in money digging. However, the fact that many of Deming's witnesses also dug for treasure does not defuse their testimony. In addition, many of the witnesses were not money diggers and passively observed both the Smiths and other neighbors in this activity. Mrs. S. F. Anderick, who described Sally Chase as a seeress, remembered Joseph Smith saying that "he could tell where lost or hidden things and treasures were buried or located with a forked witch hazel," adding that "he deceived many farmers and induced them to dig nights for chests of gold." Isaac Butts, who claimed that Joshua Stafford "told me that young Jo Smith and himself dug for money in his orchard and elsewhere nights," also described Smith's "forked witch-hazel rod with which he claimed he could locate buried money" and his "peep-stone which he put into his hat and looked into." Butts added, "I have seen both." Cornelius R. Stafford implicated John and Joshua Stafford in money digging but noted that "Jo Smith kept it up after our neighbors had abandoned it" and also repeated his uncle William's story of the sacrificed sheep. Christopher M. Stafford admitted that his stepfather and some of his neighbors had dug for money and added that Smith also searched for treasure with a witch hazel stick and peep-stone and told him "there was a peep-stone for me and many others if we could only find them." Stafford's statement is similar to a remark made by Smith to Brigham Young, and recorded in the *Latter-day Saints' Millennial Star*, that "Every man who lived on earth was entitled to a seer stone, and should have one, but they are kept from them in consequence of their wickedness, and most of those who do find one make evil use of it."[11] Christopher Stafford remembered that Smith was a "fortune teller" and "told mine by looking in the palm of my hand and said among other things that I would not live to be very old."[12]

Anderson's final objection to Deming's affidavits is that they "reveal no direct knowledge that the Smiths were involved" in money digging.[13] In order for this statement to count as true, Anderson must make two qualifications. First, by "direct knowledge" he must mean "observed actions." Second, he must exclude the testimonies of Henry A. Sawyer and W. R. Hine, both of whom claimed to have actually seen the Smiths digging for "lost and hidden things" in Pennsylvania.

To this one might answer that statements such as those of Sayer and Hine pertain to the Pennsylvania phase of Joseph Smith's career and are thus irrelevant to determining Smith's Palmyra-Manchester reputation. Such a saving distinction, however, cannot be granted for a variety of reasons. First, for at least five of the ten years that Smith lived in Manchester, he made extended visits to

Susquehanna County, Pennsylvania, where he worked for Josiah Stowell, attended school, met and courted Emma Hale, and engaged in other activities including money digging which he later admitted in the *Elders' Journal* and the *Times and Seasons*.[14] In December 1827, Smith moved to Harmony, Pennsylvania, as a permanent resident, although he often returned to his parents' home in Manchester to conduct business relative to the printing of the Book of Mormon.

Besides Smith's many peregrinations between New York and Pennsylvania, there is considerable evidence connecting his activities in the two states. In 1825, when Josiah Stowell hired Smith as a seer to help him locate buried treasure in Pennsylvania, it was because Stowell had already heard of the reputation Smith had established locally in New York as a seer of hidden treasures. Smith himself, according to reports of the "legal examination" in 1826 as a "glass looker," admitted to Justice of the Peace Albert Neely that while still at Palmyra he had by means of his stone "frequently ascertained in that way where lost property was of various kinds; that he had occasionally been in the habit of looking through this stone to find lost property for three years."[15] Martin Harris later acknowledged that Smith dug for money with Stowell not only in Pennsylvania but also in Palmyra, Manchester, and other places.[16] It is thus a contrivance to try to distinguish between Smith's New York and Pennsylvania activities.

There is another consideration which makes the Pennsylvania evidence relevant to the question of Smith's New York reputation. If, as Anderson argues, the statements taken in Palmyra-Manchester are untrustworthy because they were possibly infected by popular rumor, then statements made by people less familiar with Smith's prior reputation should be more reliable. The Pennsylvania statements, however, do not differ significantly from statements gathered a hundred miles away in Palmyra-Manchester. The charges of lying, drunkenness, and money digging occur with the same frequency and are often based on personal contact with Smith. Many charged Smith with lying because of his promise that they could see the gold plates at a specified time. Frederick Mather noted in 1880 that "All accounts agree that Smith drank freely, both in the Susquehanna and in the Harpersville neighborhoods." He provided examples of occasional inebriation related to him by Jacob Skinner.[17] Most of the Pennsylvania statements also mentioned Smith's money digging. Besides acknowledging himself a "glass looker" before a justice of the peace, Smith told Isaac Hale that "he had given up what he called 'glass-looking', and that he expected to work hard for a living and was willing to do so," a conversation also remembered by Hale's son Alva and Peter Ingersoll. Use of the same seer stone also later became important in receiving revelations and in translating the Book of Mormon.[18]

W. R. Hine's knowledge of Smith's "glass looking" was based on the sights Smith told him were revealed through the medium of the stone, including one in which Smith saw "Captain Kidd sailing on the Susquehanna River during a freshet, and that he buried two pots of gold and silver."[19] The salt spring digging described by Hine was witnessed by George Collington, who saw Smith and four other men "in the act of dodging through the woods with shovels and picks upon their shoulders, their object being to discover a salt-spring by the agency of the peek-stone."[20] Collington talked with the men, observed part of their digging, and helped perpetrate a hoax on the diggers by secretly introducing salt into the pit. A number of people, some apparently eyewitnesses, told of a dig in which Smith ordered a whole hill tunnelled through in order to immobilize a very lively treasure which "waltzed around . . . in a manner to defy the dexterity of pick and shovel."[21]

From this and other evidence it appears that Joseph Smith was viewed by many of his neighbors and contemporaries both in New York and in Pennsylvania as an occasionally intemperate village seer who led his followers in various occult adventures but produced little in the way of promised treasure.

NOTES

1. Richard L. Anderson, "Joseph Smith's New York Reputation Reappraised," *Brigham Young University Studies* 10 (Spring 1970): 300.
2. Statements of Mrs. M. C. R. Smith and C. M. Stafford, in Arthur B. Deming, *Naked Truths About Mormonism* 2 (April 1888): 1.
3. Anderson, 299, 300.
4. This was W. R. Hine, who told Deming (1:2) "that the Kelly's Mormon elders from Kirtland, called on him the day of the Ohio State election in Oct., 1884, and asked him questions and he replied, They wrote down something but did not read it to him and he does not know that it is correct."
5. Deming originally meant to preserve the originals of all his depositions but was prevented from doing so when many were lost in Chicago. Letter of A. B. Deming to A. C. Williams, 13 Jan. 1885, Painsville, Ohio, on file in the Western Reserve Historical Society.
6. There is also one statement preserved in the Western Reserve Historical Society among the A. C. Williams papers. Deming had forwarded to Williams his notes of a conversation with a Mrs. S. W. Hanson, requesting Williams to read it to her "and amend to suit her and request her signature when you have made a new copy." This Williams did, and Deming published the corrected version in the second issue of his *Naked Truths about Mormonism* (p. 3). Significantly Mrs. Hanson did not

change Deming's rough draft except to rearrange it into more orderly form.

7. Statement of E. D. Howe, 8 April 1885, Painesville, Lake County, Ohio. At the bottom is a note signed "ABD" which reads: "Two lines erased before the signature."

8. Statement of J. C. Dowen, 20 Jan. 1885, Willoughby, Lake County, Ohio.

9. A. B. Deming to A. C. Williams, 26 Jan. 1900, Philadelphia, PA; original in the Western Reserve Historical Society.

10. All of these statements appear in Deming 1:2, 3, and 2:1.

11. Ibid.; *Latter-day Saints Millennial Star* 26 (20 Feb. 1864): 118–19.

12. Stafford was nearly seventy-eight years old when he made his deposition.

13. Anderson, 301.

14. *Elders' Journal* 1 (July 1838): 43; *Times and Seasons* 3 (2 May 1842): 772.

15. [Charles Marshall], "The Original Prophet," *Fraser's Magazine* 7 (Feb. 1873): 229.

16. *Tiffany's Monthly* 5 (Aug. 1859): 164.

17. *Lippincott's Magazine* 26 (1880): 203; Mather's article, entitled "The Early Mormons: Joe Smith Operates at Susquehanna," on file in the Susquehanna Historical Society, was printed some time in 1880 in either the *Montrose Republican* or the Broome County *Republican*, but the incomplete files of these papers make exact identification impossible. The article is significant because Mather identifies his sources of information much more clearly than he did in the *Lippincott's* article.

18. See Richard S. Van Wagoner and Steven L. Walker, "Joseph Smith: The Gift of Seeing," *Dialogue: A Journal of Mormon Thought* 15 (Summer 1982): 48–68; James E. Lancaster, " 'The Gift and Power of God': The Method of Translation of the Book of Mormon," *John Whitmer Historical Association Journal* 3 (1983): 51–61; D. Michael Quinn, *Early Mormonism and the Magic World View* (Salt Lake City: Signature Books, 1986), 27–52, 112–49.

19. Hine had also looked in Smith's stone many times "and could see in it whatever I imagined."

20. *Lippincott's Magazine* 26 (1880): 202. In the *Republican* article cited above, Mather characterized Collington as a most conscientious witness who "was very careful not to appear to know overmuch about the Mormons."

21. Ibid. Other references to Smith's activities in the Colesville, Bainbridge, and Harmony areas include a letter by John Sherer, dated 18 Nov. 1830 (original in the Amistad Research Center, Dillard University, New Orleans); [A. W. Benton], "Mormonites," *Evangelical Magazine and Gospel Advocate*, 9 April 1831, 120; a letter of Joel King Noble, dated 8 March 1842 (reproduced in Walters, "From Occult to Cult with Joseph Smith, Jr.," 133–37); Emily C. Blackman, *History of Susquehanna County, Pennsylvania* (Philadelphia: Claxton, Remsen, & Haffelfinger, 1873), 577–82; the recollections of W. D. Purple in the *Chenango Union* (Norwich, NY), 2 May 1877; the exchange of letters between Hiel and Joseph Lewis and Edwin Cadwell in the *Amboy Journal*, issues of 30 April, 21 May, 4 June, 11 June, 9 July, 30 July, and 6 Aug. 1879; the Salt Lake *Daily Tribune* 23 April 1880; and Emily M. Austin, *Mormonism; or, Life among the Mormons* (Madison, WI: M. J. Cantwell, Book and Job Printer, 1882), 31–33.

Of these various sources, Emily Austin, who lived in the area from her birth in 1813 until she joined the Mormons in 1830, described Smith on his first appearance in the country as a fortune teller and money digger, and remembered one occasion in which she and her sister, Sarah Knight, visited the place where Smith, Joseph Knight, Sr., and others had dug over in their quest for buried treasure. The *Daily Tribune* article contains what is claimed to be a signed document, dated 1 November 1825, pledging Smith and others to equitable shares "if anything of value should be obtained at a certain place in Pennsylvania . . . supposed to be a valuable mine of either Gold or Silver. . . . " The *Amboy Journal* articles contain much information about Smith's activities in the Harmony area, including an abortive attempt on Smith's part to join the Methodist church in 1828. Joshua McKune and Joseph Lewis successfully contested his membership on the ground that Smith was "a practicing necromancer, a dealer in enchantments and bleeding ghosts." The *Chenango Union* article contains an account by W. D. Purple of Smith's court hearing as a "glass looker" in 1826. Purple, who attended the hearing and took notes at the request of his friend Justice Neely, repeats much of what was said on the occasion, including a moving speech by Joseph Smith, Sr., in which the old man lamented the fact that his son's "wonderful power . . . should be used only in search of filthy lucre, or its equivalent in earthly treasures. . . . " Emily Blackman recorded the testimony of some who had known Smith during his stay in Susquehanna County, and provided a detailed diagram identifying the holes Smith had ordered sunk during his association with Josiah Stowell. The letter by J. K. Noble, who was one of the justices involved in Smith's 1830 Colesville trial, contains information about Smith's money digging and describes his general character as that of "a Vagrant idler Lazy (not Drunkard) but now and then Drunk Liar Deceiver." The Benton article, like the accounts of Noble and Purple, asserts that Smith was convicted in 1826 of money digging and repeats testimony later given by Josiah Stowell demonstrating Stowell's faith in Smith's occult talents. The Rev. John Sherer's letter, written from Colesville, New York, only a few months after Smith had left the area, contains the statement: "This man has been known, in these parts, for some time, as a kind of juggler, who has pretended, through a glass, to see money under ground, &c, &c."

Chapter 6

THE KELLEY INTERVIEWS

ccording to Richard Anderson, the published account of the 1881 interviews with old citizens from the Palmyra-Manchester, New York, area conducted by Reorganized Mormons William H. and E. L. Kelley, "can be trusted as the most comprehensive investigations ever made there."[1] The reason for this is William Kelley's published report of an interview he conducted with David Whitmer, an early Mormon and one of three "witnesses" to the reality of the Book of Mormon gold plates. Because Kelley's report "is detailed and minutely agrees with known writings and comments of the Book of Mormon witness," Anderson considers it a fair test of Kelley's ability at note-taking. However, in the case of the Palmyra-Manchester interviews there is considerable disparity between Kelley's original notes and the published report based on those notes. Furthermore, Anderson has not taken into account Kelley's own possible prejudice as an apostle of the Reorganized Church of Jesus Christ of Latter Day Saints, which, like its Utah cousin, bases its faith claims on Joseph Smith's teachings. As a believer in the Book of Mormon, Kelley would have little reason to misinterpret or embellish Whitmer's testimony. But it does not necessarily follow that Kelley would retain the same impartiality when recording hostile testimony.[2]

Another consideration which lessens Kelley's reliability is the fact that he published his reconstruction of the interviews without supporting documentation. Unlike Deming, Kelley did not write up the account of his interviews at the time and then have the person interviewed read it for correctness, sign it, and have it attested by independent witnesses. Rather Kelley took only brief notes, later using these and his own memory to reconstruct what had been said. The notes themselves and the responses of some of those interviewed show that Kelley sometimes depended upon imagination as well as memory.

In his analysis of the Kelley interviews Anderson relegates the story of these negative responses to a footnote, remarking that only one interview "raises a significant issue on Kelley misquotation."[3] This judgment seems particularly inept to anyone familiar with the historical circumstances prompting the Kelley report and the reaction which followed it. About a year before the Kelley brothers visited the Palmyra-Manchester area to "hear the worst, let it hurt whom it would," there appeared in a Michigan newspaper an article purporting to contain reminiscences of the Smiths from former neighbors. These statements, collected by the Reverend C. C. Thorne, described the Smith family as "too low to associate with" and Joseph Smith as "a lazy drinking fellow, and loose in his habits in every way."[4]

The Kelleys believed these statements were "a trumped up thing" and decided to reinterview the three parties "and ascertain whether this pious Rev. told the truth about what they said or not."[5] The first of the three former neighbors they called upon was William Bryant, although for some unknown reason the Kelleys did not record having asked him about the statement he allegedly signed for Thorne. The next party they called upon was Danford Booth, to whom they reportedly posed the question:

Do you know Rev. Thorn, a Presbyterian minister at Manchester?

"Yes; I know him."

What kind of a fellow is he?

"He is a pretty sharp fellow, and will look after his bread and butter, you may depend on that."

Did he ever interview you on this subject?

"No, sir; he never did."

Did he not call to see what you knew about the Smiths and Cowderys about a year ago?

"No, he never did to my recollection."

Did you know he had a statement of yours published in Michigan in regard to this, last year?

"No, sir; I never heard of it before."

Did you ever give him one to publish?

"I never did—did not know he wanted one."

He will look out for himself, will he?

"He will that; that is him."[6]

Also among those the Kelleys called upon was Orin Reed, with whom the Kelleys reportedly had the following conversation:

Do you know Mr. Thorn, the Presbyterian minister at Manchester, over here?

"Yes, I know him slightly."

Did you not make a statement to him in regard to the character of these men; that they were low persons, and not good associates, or something of the kind?

"I never did."

Did he call on you to find out what you knew about it?

"No, sir, he never did; at least he never let me know any-thing about it, if he did."

Did you ever see a statement he sent to Michigan, last year, and had published, purporting to be what you and others knew about the Smiths and Cowderys?

"No, I never did; did not know that one was ever pub-lished before."[7]

When Orin Reed, his wife Amanda, and Danford Booth read the account of these questions and answers in the Reorganized church's official *Saints' Herald,* they promptly made affidavits before a justice of the peace accusing the Kelleys of lying.[8] Reed testified that the statement he had signed for Thorne was authentic and that "the matters set forth therein alleged to have been stated by deponent to said Thorne were so stated by deponent at the time and as mentioned in said published article." His wife, Amanda, testified that she was a witness to her husband's interview with Thorne, and "that the statements alleged to have been made by said Thorne as published in the Cadillac Mich Weekly News . . . were in fact so made, and that the lan-guage employed by her said husband was substantially as therein set forth." Danford Booth confirmed that he had been interviewed by Thorne and that the statement pub-lished by the minister was correct, and denied the Kelleys' report of his remarks about Thorne. He did not even recall their having asked him about the subject. Anderson's only remark concerning these statements is that the publication of the Kelley interviews "sparked a skirmish of affidavits." Incredibly, he denies that these affidavits cast any suspi-cion on the Kelleys as competent reporters.

The only statement Anderson does address that could raise doubts about the Kelley interviews is that of John H. Gilbert, principal typesetter for the Book of Mormon. In an affidavit Gilbert said he had been "grossly misrepresented in almost every particular, words being put into his mouth that he never uttered, and the answers to questions he did give, totally at variance from the answers given by him." In this affidavit Gilbert did not go into particulars, but in a letter to Thomas Gregg, written only days after he received William Kelley's article in the *Saints' Herald*, Gilbert claimed a number of specific errors.[9] Below are extracts from Kelley's purported interview with Gilbert and from Gilbert's letter to Gregg. Gilbert's alleged responses to Kelley are in quotation marks:

KELLEY INTERVIEW	GILBERT'S LETTER
"[Hyrum Smith] said at the time it was translated by the power of God."	[This is] utterly false. I never had any conversation with Hyrum in regard to the translation.
Why did you not change it [the Book of Mormon] and correct it? "Because they would not allow us to; they were very particular about that. We never changed it in the least. Oh, well; there might have been one or two words that I changed the spelling of; I believe I did change the spelling of one, and perhaps two, but no more."	In regard to the change of spelling two words, he words my answer entirely different from what I said to him. I told him distinctly that I changed the spelling of one word, which occurred twice in one form—no believing about it. The word changed was "travail," spelled "travel" in both instances, showing that the copyist did not know the difference.
Did you set all of the type, or did some one help you? "I did the whole of it myself, and helped to read the proof,	I did not tell him I set all the type, as he reports me saying.

too; there was no one who worked at that but myself."

"If you ever saw a Book of Mormon you will see that they changed it afterwards. . . . Here on the title page it says," (reading) " 'Joseph Smith, Jr, author and proprietor.' Afterwards, in getting out other editions they left that out, and only claimed that Joseph Smith translated it."

Well, did they claim anything else than that he was the translator when they brought the manuscript to you?

"Oh, no; they claimed that he was translating it by means of some instruments he got at the same time he did the plates, and that the Lord helped him."

"I told [Lorenzo Saunders] about [James] Cobb, of Utah, and asked him if he would send Cobb his affidavit that he saw [Sidney] Rigdon before the book was published, if he (Cobb), would write to him; he finally said he would, and I wrote to Cobb about it, and gave Saunders' address, and after a long time, I got a letter from [Cobb], saying he had written three letters to Saunders, and could get no

In regard to Smith claiming to be the author, etc., I told him I understood in later editions he only claimed to be translator, etc.; the balance of the story in regard to this authorship, is all his own coining and answering.

The long paragraph in relation to Mr. Cobb and Lorenzo Saunders is a mixed mess of truth and falsehood.

answer. I then sat down and wrote Saunders a letter myself, reminding him of his promise, and wrote to Cobb also about it; and after a long time Cobb wrote me again, that Saunders had written to him; but I have never learned how satisfactory it was, or whether he made the affidavit or not."

If you could only connect Sidney Rigdon with Smith some way, you could get up a theory [to explain the Book of Mormon].

"Yes; that is just where the trouble lies; . . . But I think I have got a way out of the difficulty now. A fellow that used to be here, by the name of Saunders, Lorenzo Saunders, was back here some time ago, and I was asking him about it. At first he said he did not remember of ever seeing Rigdon until after 1830 sometime; but after studying it over a while, he said it seemed to him that one time he was over to Smiths, and that there was a stranger there he never saw before, and that they said it was Rigdon."

When I asked Mr. S[aunders] if he knew whether [Sidney] Rigdon was hanging around Smith previous to the publication of the M[ormon] B[ible], he said, "Yes, at least eighteen months before." There was no hesitancy about it; and this is what I told Kelley. You can see how he reported the matter.

What will you take for your copy of the Book of Mormon; or will you sell it? . . .
"I will take Five Hundred Dollars for it, and no less; I have known them to sell for more than that."

I did not tell Kelley that I had known a copy or copies of the M.B. to sell for $500, or more than that; that is one of his misrepresentations.

"Oh, I don't think the Smiths were as bad as people let on for. Now Tucker, in his work, told too many big things; nobody could believe his stories."

What he charges me with saying about the Smiths and Tucker's book, is all his own coining.

[From the interview with Hyram Jackway:]
"Joe and his father got drunk once. . . . "
What did they drink to make them drunk?
"They drank cider."
Got drunk so they could not walk, on cider, did they?

Mr. Jackaway tells me he did not tell Kelley that Joe and his father got drunk on cider, but on whiskey.

In a footnote Anderson observes that Gilbert's letter "is a source of confirmation of the basic accuracy of the Kelley reports." He writes: "Without claiming perfection for the Kelleys (or any other nineteenth-century interview), one can see that Gilbert admits the main direction of conversation, and quarrels with certain details. Some of Gilbert's 'misrepresentations' are trivial."[10]

Considered as an answer to Gilbert's letter, this statement is inadequate. Gilbert never denied that the Kelleys contacted him and asked certain questions; rather, he charged them with putting words in his mouth and reporting answers differently from those he in fact gave them.

Anderson has done nothing to correct this except to note that some of Gilbert's denials are "trivial," an implicit admission that others are not. The larger issue of William Kelley's accuracy in reporting the words of others is ignored, while readers are left with the impression that Gilbert's criticisms of Kelley misquotations are insignificant.

Actually, even Gilbert's most "trivial" corrections are not wholly irrelevant to the issue of Kelley misquotations. The errors Gilbert alleges might be unimportant if the Kelleys had claimed to report only the gist of their conversation, but both claimed far more than that. William emphasized that the interviews were reprinted "just as they occurred," and his brother later remarked that the language of those interviewed "was taken down at the time—the parties own words."[11] Gilbert's complaints are thus serious ones. If what he says is correct, either the Kelleys were exceptionally poor note-takers or they were exaggerating when they claimed to be reporting the exact words of those interviewed.

It now seems apparent that the Kelleys were guilty on both counts. The notes from which they constructed these interviews are on file in the archives of the Reorganized Church of Jesus Christ of Latter Day Saints in Independence, Missouri. These notes consist mainly of brief entries only a few words long and are rarely sufficiently comprehensive to give a respondent's exact words. For example, only about one hundred words were used to construct Gilbert's lengthy interview, often brief entries like "James L. Cob of Salt Lake corresponds with Colonel Gilbert."[12] From this the Kelleys constructed the lengthy paragraph which Gilbert later branded "a mixed mess of truth and falsehood." Statements Gilbert claimed he never made do not appear in the notes, and others are so abbreviated as to be all but useless in accurately reconstructing conversations. Such inadequate methodology characterizes the reporters Anderson praises for their precise note-taking abilities.

Many of William Kelley's errors can be ascribed to simple carelessness. Equipped only with his inadequate notes, Kelley was forced to rely on his own evidently often unreliable memory to retrieve the information. Vaguely recalling that Gilbert had qualified his remark about not changing the Book of Mormon, Kelley no doubt added the account of changing one or two words, forgetting that Gilbert had said he changed the spelling of one word.[13] Possessing the brief note, "Major Gilbert of Palmyra Sat up the type of B. of M.,"[14] Kelley interpreted this to mean that Gilbert alone had set the type, which Gilbert refuted.[15] Kelley's errors in reporting Gilbert's statements about Cobb and the cost of an original edition of the Book of Mormon are probably related to the same problem of abbreviated notes and imprecise memory.

Kelley's note-taking and faulty memory may thus explain some of Gilbert's charges, but they do not excuse all of them. In fact, Gilbert called Kelley a "great falsifier" and "the champion liar of America" and charged him in an affidavit with gross and willful falsification.[16] A further comparison of Gilbert's letter and the Kelley notes tends to support Gilbert's allegation. For example, according to Kelley, Gilbert maintained that the Smiths were not "as bad as people let on" and that Tucker "told too many big things; nobody could belive his stories." Gilbert denied having said this and nothing appears in Kelley's notes which might have prompted such a recollection. Either Kelley was remembering something Gilbert said but could not remember, which is unlikely considering how carefully Kelley recorded in his notes each and every favorable mention of the Smiths, or Kelley created the exchange for the express purpose of increasing the number of witnesses who did not share the prevailing opinion of the family. Add to this the fact that Gilbert was interviewed many times on the subject of Mormonism, and that in none of these did he venture an opinion of the Smiths like that attributed to him by Kelley, and it becomes evident that the remark cannot be assigned to Gilbert as an authentic reflection of his views. It seems more likely that Gilbert said nothing about the Smiths' general reputation, a silence which Kelley interpreted to mean he thought well of the family.

This tendency to "interpret" his witnesses in order to have them say things that in Kelley's estimation should have been said is evident in other parts of his interview with Gilbert. For example, in that part of the interview in which Gilbert and Kelley supposedly discussed the question of whether Smith claimed to be "translator" or "author" of the Book of Mormon, Gilbert is made to bring up the objection that Smith changed the title page of the Book of Mormon. To this Kelley responded, "Well, did they claim anything else than that he was the translator when they brought the manuscript to you?" Gilbert answered in the negative, thus disposing of one common objection to the Book of Mormon. The argument appears even tighter when the reader remembers Gilbert's earlier remark about Hyrum Smith claiming that the book had been "translated by the power of God."

The problem with this exchange has nothing to do with the merits of Kelley's argument; rather, the question is whether Gilbert said any such thing as Kelley alleges. Gilbert admitted that he made a remark about Smith claiming in later editions to be only the "translator" of the Book of Mormon, but claimed that "the balance of the story in regard to this authorship, is all his [Kelley's] own coining and answering." He further denied having had any conversation with Hyrum Smith about the translation, which if true means that Kelley indulged in dramatic license to make a point. Gilbert's remembered remark about the change on the title page of the Book of Mormon gave Kelley an opportunity to refute what was then a common objection to the book, and it apparently mattered little to him whether he and Gilbert had actually discussed the matter. The opportunity to confound his critics was simply too good to miss.

If Kelley was writing a dramatic dialogue whose primary purpose was to persuade and convince, there would of course be no question concerning the propriety of such an argument. Kelley, however, was writing a report professing to be a sober recital of facts "just as they occurred." He did allow "for a possible mistake, or error, arising from a misapprehension, or mistake in taking notes,"[17] but he did not grant himself the freedom to have those interviewed say what could or should have been said. It was probably for this reason that Kelley did not afford those interviewed the chance to read or confirm their testimonies. If Kelley had wanted to gather only authentic information, he would probably have granted his informants this courtesy.

Another example of Kelley's manipulation can be seen in his report of Hyram Jackway's story about Joseph Smith's drinking. According to that report, Jackway remembered seeing Smith and his father drunk in a hayfield. "What did they drink to make them drunk?" Kelley asked. "They drank cider," Jackway answered. To this Kelley replied, "Got drunk so they could not walk, on cider, did they?" Kelley here implied that Jackway was exaggerating, since cider was not generally classified at the time as an "ardent spirit." According to Gilbert, however, Jackway said the Smiths did not get "drunk on cider, but on whiskey."

Gilbert's letter suggests a tendency on the part of Kelley to "play down" any statement potentially harmful to his faith. In discussing the origin of the Book of Mormon, for example, Kelley has Gilbert express considerable uncertainty about the testimony of Lorenzo Saunders, who

Gilbert names as his source for the theory that Sidney Rigdon helped Smith write the Book of Mormon. According to Kelley's rendering of the conversation, Gilbert said that Saunders initially could not remember seeing Rigdon with Smith before the book came off the press in 1830, and only "remembered" seeing the two men together before that time after repeated promptings by Gilbert. Why Kelley should choose to report the conversation in this way when Gilbert said that Saunders responded promptly, with none of the "hesitancy" reported by Kelley, was obviously to discredit the then dominant theory that Smith had help in writing the Book of Mormon. By altering Gilbert's words Kelley provided readers with a good reason to discount the theory on the basis of one of its chief exponent's own admissions.

It is, of course, possible that Saunders was mistaken in his recollection, but there is little ground for supposing that the mistake—if mistake it was—was due to Gilbert's having planted the idea in the first place. The notes from which Kelley constructed this part of the interview read simply, "Lorenzo Saunders says Rigdon was in the neighborhood before B of M was published 18 months."[18] There is nothing here indicating the uncertainty Gilbert allegedly attributed to Saunders, nor does Gilbert, in a letter he wrote some months before his interview with Kelley, indicate hesitancy on the part of Saunders: "says he knows that Rigdon was hanging around Smith's for eighteen months prior to the publishing of the Mormon Bible."[19] Finally, in 1885 and 1887 Saunders himself wrote two statements in which he described his alleged meeting with Rigdon in the spring of 1827, and in neither did he hint that he was less than certain about the recollection.[20]

There is additional evidence which throws light on Gilbert's conversation with Saunders. On 17 September 1884, William Kelley was in Reading, Michigan, and there

spoke with Lorenzo Saunders himself about his knowledge
of the Smith family and his memory of seeing Rigdon in
Palmyra before 1830. On this occasion Kelley was consid-
erably more careful than he had been in the past, for he
wrote out the report on the spot and had Saunders sign it
as being correct.

Kelley asked Saunders if he had seen Rigdon in
the Smiths' neighborhood before 1830, and Saunders answered, "Yes. In March 1827." Kelley asked if Saunders
knew Gilbert, to which he replied, "Yes. Four years ago I
went to Palmyra to see my Brothers, and I met Gilbert. He
wanted to know if I remembered seeing Sidney Rigdon in
that neigh-borhood previous to 1830 when he come preach-
ing the Mormon Bible. . . . Says I to Gilbert Sidney Rigdon
was about Smiths before 1830 in my opinion. Gilbert asked
me if I would make affidavit that I saw Rigdon at Smiths
before that time? I told him I would think the matter
over. . . . When I got ready to come home Gilbert said he
wanted to see me before I left. . . . He came to me as I was
about to start home and it was then that I told him that I
had thought the matter over and made up my mind that I
could swear that I saw Rigdon in the neighborhood in the
spring of 1827."[21]

Two observations should be made concerning
Saunders's statement. First, there is no mention of
Saunders's initial inability to remember seeing Rigdon before 1830. He answered Kelley promptly and remembered
saying to Gilbert, "I saw Rigdon in the neighborhood in
the spring of 1827." Had Kelley been able to persuade
Saunders to admit that he could not initially remember seeing Rigdon before 1830, Kelley would certainly have done
so. But Saunders was firm in his recollection despite Kelley's
questions about the time, place, and circumstances of the
alleged meeting. Second, in Kelley's published report of
his conversation with Gilbert, Gilbert is said to have men-

tioned that Saunders hesitated and implies that Saunders was trying to remember something he could not remember. According to Saunders, he "studied it over" before committing to an affidavit because he wanted to be certain of the date. When he recalled the exact circumstances of their meeting, he felt confident enough to appear before a magistrate. Of course the issue is not whether Saunders's recollection was correct but whether Kelley represented correctly what Gilbert said about Saunders's recollection. Gilbert denied the suggestion that Saunders could not initially remember seeing Rigdon, and none of his or Saunders's various statements indicate that Gilbert was lying. Significantly Kelley made no effort to publish the report of his own interview with Lorenzo Saunders.

When E. L. Kelley was told of Gilbert's affidavit charging William Kelley with misrepresentation, he responded by calling Gilbert a liar. "The fact is," he said, "Major Gilbert, if he made that affidavit, lied, and I know that he did. I am willing to face him in Palmyra, or any other place, and say that it is not true because I know his language was taken down at the time." Gilbert, he continued, "does not state a single thing wherein he has been misrepresented. Was it in the statement that he had been trying for fifty years to collect evidence against the Book of Mormon? Was it in that he said he had a way out of the difficulty now he thought; that he had spoken to Saunders to testify that Rigdon was there, and afterwards had written him, but Saunders had not received it? Was it in that he is reported as disbelieving in the Bible?"[22]

A number of objections can be raised against Kelley's rebuttal. First, Kelley was there with his brother at the original interview, so he must have been aware of some inaccuracies in the published report. Second, if Kelley's list of guesses as to what specific charges Gilbert had in mind reflects Kelley's own memory of the conversation, his statement confirms rather than denies Gilbert's version of the exchange. Gilbert's list of claimed misrepresentations does not include one specific item mentioned by Kelley. Finally, there is no evidence that Gilbert ever told less than the truth on the subject of Mormonism. If one deletes the remarks Gilbert denied making, he told Kelley the same story he had repeated on many occasions—a story he did not embellish despite many opportunities to do so. Nor was Gilbert, as Kelley alleges, one who would defend a popular cause at the price of his own honesty. He never pretended to know more than he actually did about the origin of Mormonism and once repudiated a statement which, if true, would have lent credibility to the claim that Joseph Smith was a fraud.[23]

Gilbert was not the only one to charge Kelley with misrepresentation. Three others accused him of taking undue liberties with their words. Further evidence suggests that at least two others may have been similarly dissatisfied. In answer to the objection that this only proves collusion on the part of Kelley's critics are Kelley's own notes. These demonstrate that the complaints of Gilbert, Danford Booth, and Orin and Amanda Reed were not contrived, for comparing Kelley's notes with his published reports provides independent support for the same accusations.

Gilbert's first accusation was that Kelley's report was anything but a stenographic record giving the respondents' "exact language taken at the time; written in their presence."[24] Conversations containing thousands of words in Kelley's published report were reconstructed from notes of not more than fifty words, notes often not even mentioning subjects addressed in the published report. In the published interview with Ezra Pierce, for example, Kelley asks about Joseph Smith's drinking, education, money digging, and alleged counterfeiting. In addition, he also engages Pierce in a long theological debate from which Kelley emerges the winner. However, in the forty-seven words "taken at the time," there is no hint of talk about theology, money digging, or counterfeiting. All, it appears, are topics introduced by Kelley to show his religion in the best possible light, demonstrating not only the theological superiority of his faith but the duplicity of those who make unsupported accusations against Smith. Even if these additions could be ascribed to Kelley's memory, the question still remains of just what Pierce actually said. As will be shown below, there are serious questions concerning Kelley's accuracy even in reporting statements based on his own notes.

Kelley's notes provide abundant evidence that he was guilty of deliberate misreporting when the subject was Joseph Smith's character—especially the matter of Smith's and his associates' alleged intemperance. For example, Kelley's published interview reports that he asked Danford Booth if Oliver Cowdery drank, and Booth replied, "Every body drank then. I never saw Cowdery drink."[25] In his notes, Kelley only wrote, "Was Cowdry a drunkard[?] Every body drank then."[26] The printed version corrects the implication in the notes that Cowdery drank along with everyone else by adding, "I never saw Cowdery drink."

In other interviews Kelley substituted "drink" for the word "drunk" which appeared in his notes, a substitution which often resulted in a significant change of meaning. For example, in the published version, William Bryant answers "no" to Kelley's question, "Did you ever see Joe Smith drunk, or drinking?"[27] But according to Kelley's notes, Bryant only said that he had never seen Smith drunk—not that he had never seen Smith drinking. A similar change occurs in Kelley's interview with Ezra Pierce. Kelley's notes show that Pierce said he "Has pulled sticks with Joes for a gallon of Brandy but never knew [him] to get drunk."[28] In the published article, this notation is expanded into a long question-and-answer exchange in which Pierce volunteers the information that "Every body drank them times" but that he had never seen "young Joe drink."[29] Again the substitution of the word "drink" for "drunk" changes the meaning of the exchange.[30]

Kelley deviated most from his notes when respondents said something Kelley interpreted as being clearly detrimental to the character of Joseph Smith or his associates. According to Kelley's notes, Mary Bryant said, "Cowdrys were low shacks." Danford Booth called Oliver Cowdery a "low pettefogging lawer."[31] These statements were similar to those collected by the Rev. Thorne, and Kelley did not let them stand unadorned. In the published interview Bryant is made to emphatically claim that Lyman Cowdery and his family were the only Cowderys she ever knew. Since Lyman Cowdery was never a Mormon or even very sympathetic to Mormonism, such a claim did not damage the faith. Booth's description of "O. Cowdery" as a "low pettefogging lawer" was also transmuted into a statement about Lyman Cowdery. In addition, Booth was made to explain that by "pettifogger" he did not mean a trickster but rather a lawyer who "took small cases and practiced before justices of the peace. We call them pettifoggers here."[32] This explanation removed much of the sting from the statement Orin Reed supposedly made for Rev. Thorne, "I was acquainted with Oliver Cowdery. He was a low pettifogger, the cat's-paw of the Smiths to do their dirty work."[33]

However brief and incomplete, Kelley's notes were still sometimes too complete for his purposes. Two comments appear in his notes which find no parallel in the published report, probably because Kelley found both offensive. In John Stafford's generally favorable report, he said, according to Kelley's notes, "[Smith] was a little contentious but never saw him fight—known him to scuffle."[34] In the published report, Stafford says only, "Never saw him fight; have known him to scuffle."[35] The phrase "he was a little contentious" would have spoiled what Richard Anderson later interpreted as "the distinction between brawling and playful wrestling."[36] Kelley also deleted the latter part of Gilbert's statement, "Harris was a very honest farmer but very superstitious—He saw the Book with his spiritual eyes."[37] Since anti-Mormon writers had long been using Martin Harris's comment about witnessing the Book of Mormon gold plates in a vision to cast doubt upon the objective reality of the plates, Kelley simply removed the comment.[38]

Another problem is Kelley's marked tendency to "improve" statements reflecting favorably on the Smiths. For example, in the notes of his conversation with Thomas Taylor, Kelley recorded only, "Says nothing has been sustained against Smith."[39] From this Kelley constructed a lengthy panegyric which even Smith's most devoted followers would have been hard-pressed to match. Smith's only fault, according to Kelley's Taylor, was that he was "ahead of the people." "There was something about him they could not understand; some way he knew more than they did, and it made them mad." The Smiths were hated because they had "the manhood to stand up for their own convictions," and those who claim otherwise are nothing more than "a set of d— —d liars" who "love a lie better than the truth." Smith's story of the gold plates Taylor also unhesitatingly affirmed: "Right over here, in Illinois and Ohio, in mounds there, they have discovered copper plates since, with hieroglyphics all over them; and quite a number of the old settlers around here testified that Smith showed the plates to them—they were good, honest men, and what is the sense in saying they lied?" Kelley does add a disclaimer of sorts, for Taylor is a non-Mormon: "Now, I never saw the Book of Mormon—don't know anything about it, nor care."[40] This is the same statement Kelley had put in the mouth of Orlando Saunders when he, too, had waxed overly enthusiastic.

Anderson's argument that the Kelley report provides a reliable source for contemporary information about Joseph Smith has been thoroughly discredited. Kelley claimed to be reporting the facts "impartially—just as they occurred—the good and the bad, side by side," yet he deleted or amended derogatory remarks, embellished or deliberately created favorable recollections, and sometimes invented dialogue. He claimed that his report was a verbatim transcript, when in fact it was a reconstruction based partly on notes, partly on memory, and partly on a determined will to discredit Philastus Hurlbut.

While Kelley's published report may contain more hagiography than history, his notes are of particular interest in relationship to the evidence gathered by Hurlbut. Despite the differences in purpose of the two men, and the differences of opinion between the people they contacted, the fact is that their witnesses rarely dissented from each other on specific grounds of experience. For example, according to Kelley's notes of those asked about the Smiths' drinking habits, two replied that the Smiths drank but they did not remember seeing them drunk, one did remember seeing Joseph Smith and his father "Drunk in a hay field," and another recalled Joseph Smith getting drunk on boiled cider.[41] A number said that the Smiths were good workers if hired by someone else but if left to themselves were "shiftless" and "poor managers."[42]

On the matter of the Smiths' money digging, only one witness claimed to know anything about it, and he told much the same story as Hurlbut's witnesses. Dr. John Stafford, who probably knew more about the Smiths than anyone else interviewed by Kelley, recalled that "old Joe claimed he understood Geology and could tell all kinds of minerals," and he remembered an unsuccessful attempt by Lucy Smith to borrow his father's seer stone.[43] When asked about his personal knowledge of the Smiths' money digging, he responded, "Smiths with others were hunting for money previous to obtaining plates. . . . Saw them dig 3 or 4 years before B[ook] was found—Joe not there."[44] Stafford may here be referring to the same dig described by his father nearly fifty years before. On that occasion Joseph Smith was not at the digging site but supervising from the house, "looking in his stone and watching the motions of the evil spirit."[45]

Stafford was hardly the kind of malicious gossip-monger which Anderson denominates Hurlbut's witnesses. Stafford in fact called Joseph Smith "a real clevy [clever] jovial boy" and thought Pomeroy Tucker's derogatory comments on the family "false absolutely."[46] But he agreed with Tucker that Smith was a money digger who sometimes drank too much.

Nor was Stafford alone in his opinion. When Frederick Mather traveled to Pennsylvania in 1880 to interview people there who had known Joseph Smith, four of the nine people he talked with regarded Smith as "a good and kind neighbor," but many of these same people stated that he was also an intemperate and superstitious money digger. Clearly when sympathetic and antagonistic witnesses tend to agree on a story, there is every reason to accept that story as true.

One report which Anderson claims cannot be reconciled with Hurlbut's early affidavits is the statement of Orlando Saunders, who described the Smiths as good workers and "the best family in the neighborhood in case of sickness."[47] Saunders's report is certainly valuable for emphasizing the Smith family's charity, but it does not conflict with statements collected by Hurlbut. The Smith family could have been involved in money digging and still have been "kind in sickness." Similarly, the fact that Saunders did not mention money digging does not mean that the Smiths were not money diggers. Kelley may not have asked Saunders about money digging or he may have failed to record an answer.

Saunders's statement that the Smiths were "good fellows to work" also does not contradict Hurlbut's accusation of shiftlessness in connection with their money digging. If Saunders's contact with the family predated their most intensive money-digging period, then his claim harmonizes with the statement of Joshua Stafford, who recorded that the Smiths "were laboring people" until sometime after they "commenced digging for hidden treasures."[48] But it is not necessary to thus limit Saunders's contact in order to harmonize the reports. Hurlbut's witnesses did not accuse the Smiths of unqualified laziness. As several reports make clear, the Smiths were considered "indolent" not because they were idlers but because they devoted a disproportionate share of their time to the profitless business of money digging. They seemed, at least to their neighbors, more interested in pursuing "visionary projects" than in successfully earning a traditional living.

While much of what Saunders said about the Smiths is not strictly in conflict with Hurlbut's description of the family, there still remain some remarks which resist harmonization. In every case, however, these seemingly irreconcilable statements cannot definitely be ascribed to Saunders. For example, Anderson cites one of Saunders's comments in order to disprove "the Hurlbut contention that the Book of Mormon was Joseph Smith's inconsistent adaptation of his treasure seeking,"[49] but the statement he cites cannot be located among the notes Kelley took at the time of the original interview. Anderson also quotes an alleged recollection as evidence that the Smiths paid their debts, but again the statement is found only in the printed version of Kelley's interview with Saunders.[50] Considering Kelley's "evident editorializing talents," such remarks are clearly of little value unless confirmed by independent evidence.

Despite Kelley's attempt to "improve" on Saunders's recollection, there is still no reason to think that Saunders's opinion of the Smiths was less than favorable. This, however, in no way supports Anderson's contention that Hurlbut's witnesses are untrustworthy; it only shows that Saunders's experience differed on some points from theirs. Clearly, because a witness like Saunders found the Smiths industrious and temperate does not prove them to have been so at all times and in all places, just as the fact that those who saw them drunk when they should have been working does not prove them always to have been drunken laggards. It seems more likely that all of these witnesses were telling the truth insofar as they knew it, and that the Smiths are simply being described from the particular perspective of the witnesses' contact with the family. Saunders's recollection that the Smiths drank but never got drunk means only that they never got drunk in his presence, which of course does not mean that a witness like C. M. Stafford was lying when he claimed to have seen Smith drunk often, especially since he recalled one specific incident also described by Barton and John Stafford.

The same may be said of Saunders's and Stafford's recollections of the Smiths' working habits. Saunders described the male Smiths as "good workers" and singled out Samuel Smith as the best; Stafford also called Samuel an "industrious boy" but remembered Joseph Smith as "the laziest one of the family." Stafford may only have meant that Joseph was not as diligent a worker as his brother, but Stafford had other reasons for this opinion.

On two separate occasions Smith had had too much to drink while working with Stafford, which would hardly recommend him as a dependable worker in Stafford's eyes.

In this same regard it is interesting to compare Orlando Saunders's impressions of the Smiths with those of his brother Lorenzo, who knew the Smiths equally well but did not share Orlando's favorable opinion of the family. Orlando remembered Lucy Smith primarily because of her kindness during his father's illness, but Lorenzo was also impressed with the fact that she "could not tell a straight story" and was "industrious but nasty," evidently referring to the type of work she sometimes did. Orlando mentioned the elder Smith only in passing, but Lorenzo remembered him as a profoundly superstitious man who "would go to turkey shoots and get drunk pretend to enchant their guns so they could not kill a turkey." Orlando did not refer to Joseph Smith except to include him with the other Smiths as a good worker, but Lorenzo recalled meeting him on a number of specific occasions. He described Smith's seer stone and recalled asking him if "he could not look into futurity? Joe said he could not look into any holy thing." Orlando admitted that he had never seen them digging for money but claimed he once witnessed them digging in a hill "said to be for that purpose; that young Joe could look in his Peep Stone and see a man sitting in a gold chair. Old Joe said he was King i.e. the man in the chair; a King of one of the tribes, who was shut in there in the time of one of their big battles." Lorenzo agreed with his brother that the Smiths "were pretty good fellows in their way" but in his opinion were not respectable because "they were shiftless and were in the money digging business."[51]

The unanimity of contemporary, firsthand opinion on these two points—money digging and drinking—from the Smith family's closest acquaintances is impressive. Lorenzo Saunders thought that Joseph Smith, Sr., drank too much and that his son Joseph Jr. was a shiftless money digger. Isaac Butts and Christopher M. Stafford, who both attended school with Joseph Jr. and worked with him on numerous occasions, described the elder Smith as a drunkard and his namesake as a frequently intoxicated money digger. Isaac Hale, who perhaps knew Joseph Smith as well if not better than anyone outside Smith's immediate family, condemned his son-in-law as a money-digging imposter. And Hale's son Alva, who knew Joseph Smith almost as well, shared his father's opinion, adding that he believed Smith proved himself dishonest when he backed out of his promise to show Hale the gold plates.

Although the impressions of Joseph Smith by his early acquaintances are phrased in subjective, sometimes hostile language, they are not, as Richard Anderson maintains, contradictory. Anderson's assumption that complimentary reports negate what he sees as derogatory comments is unconvincing.[52] If our intent is the beatification of the young Joseph Smith, we may suspect collusion among dishonest witnesses. But if we are willing to accept the reminiscences at face value, as all available evidence suggests, we can clearly see the surprise and resentment of neighbors who saw in Smith a nondescript, even disreputable, young man from a poor family who had sent himself up as the leader of a new religious movement.

NOTES

1. Richard L. Anderson, "Joseph Smith's New York Reputation Reappraised," *Brigham Young University Studies* 10 (Spring 1970): 305.
2. *The Saints' Herald* 29 (March 1882): 68.
3. Anderson, 305n47.
4. *Cadillac* (MI) *Weekly News*, 6 April 1880, in E. L. Kelley and Clark Braden, *Public Discussion of the Issues Between the Reorganized Church of Jesus Christ of Latter Day Saints and the Church of*

Christ (Disciples) . . . (St. Louis: Christian Publishing Co., 1884), 119. I have been unable to locate an original copy of this newspaper.
5. William H. Kelley, "The Hill Cumorah . . . The Stories of Hurlbert, Howe, Tucker, &c. From Later Interviews," *Saints' Herald* 28 (1 June 1881): 162.
6. Ibid., 162–63.
7. Ibid., 165.
8. The following affidavits are copied from the originals in the Ontario County Clerk's Office:

State of New York
County of Ontario
    Danforth Booth, of the town of Manchester in said County, being duly affirmed deposes and says, that he has read the article published in the Cadillac Mich Weekly news of April 6, 1880, respecting "Cowdery and the Smith family" over the signature of C. C. Thorne, that the interview therein mentioned, between deponent and said Thorne, did in fact take place, and that the matters set forth therein, alleged to have been stated by deponent to said Thorne were so stated by deponent.
    Deponent further says that he has read a paper called the "Saints Herald" purporting to give an interview between one Wm H Kelley and another person and deponent, in which they state that deponent informed them that said Thorne and deponent never had an interview as alleged by said Thorne. Deponent says that he did not so inform them, and has no recollection of such question being asked him.
[Signed] D. Booth

Subscribed and affirmed
to before me July 1, 1881
    N. K. Cole
    Justice of the Peace

State of New York
County of Ontario
    Orrin Reed of the town of Manchester, in said County be-

ing duly affirmed, deposes and says, –that his age is 77 years, –that he was born in the town of Farmington, and about four miles from Mormon Hill (so called) that for forty six years last past he has resided in said town Manchester, and in the same school district in which Joseph Smith, and family–of Mormon notoriety–resided and three fourths of a mile from Mormon Hill aforesaid. Deponent says that he has read the article published in the Cadillac (Mich) Weekly News of April 6, 1880, respecting "Cowdery and the Smith family" over the signature of C. C. Thorne, –that the matters set forth therein alleged to have been stated by deponent to said Thorne were so stated by deponent at the time and as mentioned in said published article.

[Signed] Orin Reed

Affirmed and subscribed
to before me June 29, 1881
    N. K. Cole
    Justice of the Peace

State of New York
County of Ontario
    Amanda Reed being duly affirmed deposes and says that she is the wife of Orin Reed, whose deposition appears above, that she was present and heard a conversation between her said husband and C. C. Thorne–that the statements alleged to have been made by said Thorne as published in the Cadillac Mich Weekly News, over the signature of said Thorne were in fact so made, and that the language employed by her said husband was substantially as therein set forth.

[Signed] Amanda Reed

Affirmed and subscribed
to before me June 29, 1881
    N. K. Cole
    Justice of the Peace

9. Letter dated 19 June 1881, Palmyra, NY, in Charles A. Shook, *The True Origin of Mormon Polygamy* (Cincinnati: The Standard Publishing Co., 1914), 37–38.
10. Anderson, 305.

11. Kelley, "Interviews," 168; *Braden and Kelley Debate*, 122.
12. Kelley, "Notes," back of p. 9, archives, Reorganized Church of Jesus Christ of Latter Day Saints, Independence, Missouri.
13. Compare Gilbert's letter to Cobb, 10 Feb. 1879, Palmyra, Wayne County, NY: "In one instance he [Cowdery] was looking over the manuscript, when the word 'travail' occurred twice in the form, but spelled in the manuscript *travel*. Mr. Grandin when reading the proof pronounced the word correctly, but Cowdery did not seem to know the difference." Original in the New York Public Library. Gilbert also alluded to this same change in a letter to Clark Braden, dated Palmyra, 27 Feb. 1884, in *Braden and Kelley Debate*, 382.
14. Kelley, "Notes," back of p. 5.
15. In numerous statements, Gilbert was careful to explain that he did not set all of the type. See, for example, the *Detroit Post & Tribune*, 3 Dec. 1877.
16. In his 27 February 1884 letter to Braden, Gilbert maintained: "Mr. Kelley misrepresented me in every important particular in his article. . . . If Mr. Kelley has to resort to falsehood and mis-representation to defend Mormonism, he had better leave them and become an honest man if possible."
17. Kelley, "Interviews," 168.
18. Kelley, "Notes," 9.
19. Letter of J. H. Gilbert to James T. Cobb, dated Palmyra, 14 Oct. 1879, in William Wyl, *Mormon Portraits . . .* (Salt Lake City: Tribune Printing & Publishing Co., 1886), 231.
20. Saunders's statements appeared in Charles A. Shook, *The True Origin of the Book of Mormon* (Cincinnati: The Standard Publishing Co., 1914), 134–35; and Arthur B. Deming, *Naked Truths About Mormonism* 1 (Jan. 1888): 2.
21. Unpublished statement of Lorenzo Saunders, 2, 4–5, 13, RLDS church archives.
22. *Braden and Kelley Debate*, 123.
23. Gilbert to James T. Cobb, 16 March 1879; original in New York Public Library. Gilbert refuted the statement of J. N. T. Tucker, first published in the *Signs of the Times*, 8 June 1842, and later in John C. Bennett, *The History of the Saints . . .*

(Boston: Leland & Whiting, 1842), 123.

24. *Braden and Kelley Debate*, 122.
25. Kelley, "Interviews," 162.
26. Kelley, "Notes," 3.
27. Kelley, "Interviews," 162.
28. Kelley, "Notes," 4.
29. Kelley, "Interviews," 163.
30. Another example of Kelley's manner of handling the charge of drinking occurs in his interview with Abel Chase. According to the published article, Chase said nothing about the Smiths' drinking habits, but in Kelley's notes appears the entry, "Every one drank" (p. 10). Since this comment immediately follows a list of the members of the Smith family (which in the article is taken from the mouth of Chase and put into the mouth of Orlando Saunders, evidently to make the sympathetic Saunders appear to know the Smiths better than the unsympathetic Chase), it probably refers to the Smiths' collective drinking habits, not those of their neighbors.
31. Kelley, "Notes," 2, 3.
32. Kelley, "Interview," 162. It is possible that Bryant and Booth were confusing Lyman with Oliver Cowdery, but nothing appears in Kelley's notes to indicate this. It appears that Kelley decided to have his witnesses correct themselves rather than correcting them by way of editorial comment. In this way Kelley could remove the bite from such remarks yet still claim his interviews were published "without comment."
33. *Cadillac Weekly News*, 6 April 1880, in *Braden and Kelley Debate*, 119.
34. Kelley, "Notes," 14.
35. Kelley, "Interviews," 167.
36. Anderson, 306.
37. Kelley, "Notes," 10.
38. Gilbert repeated Harris's remark at least three times to others, once in his 16 March 1879 letter to Cobb (original in New York Public Library), once in a memorandum dated 8 September 1892 (original in the Palmyra King's Daughters Free

Library, Inc.), and again in an interview reported in the *New York Herald*, 25 June 1893. Other references to Harris's statement are found in John A. Clark, *Gleanings by the Way* (Philadelphia: W. J. & J. K. Simon, 1842), 256–57; Pomeroy Tucker, *The Origin, Rise and Progress of Mormonism* (New York: D. Appleton & Co., 1867), 71, 290; *Braden and Kelley Debate*, 173; A. Deming, *Naked Truths About Mormonism* 2 (April 1888):1, 3; A. Metcalf, *Ten Years Before the Mast. . . .* (Malad, ID: By the Author, 1888), 70; and Stephen Burnett's letter to Lyman E. Johnson, 15 April 1838, Orange Township, Geauga County, Ohio, archives, historical department, Church of Jesus Christ of Latter-day Saints, Salt Lake City, Utah. For evidence that David Whitmer may have held much the same opinion, see Emily Dickinson, *New Light on Mormonism* (New York: Funk & Wagnalls, 1885), 261–62, and Gene A. Sessions, ed., *A View of James Henry Moyle: His Diaries and Letters* (Salt Lake City: n.p., 1974), 28–30.

39. Kelley, "Notes," 1.
40. Kelley, "Interviews," 167.
41. Kelley, "Notes," 11, back of p. 13.
42. Ibid., 7, 14.
43. Ibid., back of p. 14, 15, back of p. 13. Compare this last recollection to the statement of Samantha Payne, "She [Lucy Smith] once came to my mother to get a stone the children had found, of curious shape. She wanted to use it as a peepstone." Cited in *Braden and Kelley Debate*, 350.
44. Ibid., 13, back of p. 15. Kelley changed little of this when preparing his report for publication except to weaken the force of Stafford's recollection by inserting a qualifying, "I think," into his account of seeing the Smiths in a treasure dig. Anderson pounces upon this phrase as casting doubt on Stafford's recollection.
45. William Stafford also dates this dig as occurring some time before the Smiths "pretended to find a gold bible." Eber D. Howe, *Mormonism Unvailed . . .* (Painesville, OH: Printed and published by the author, 1834), 239.
46. Kelley, "Notes," 13.

47. Ibid., 6.
48. Howe, 258.
49. Anderson, 309.
50. In Kelley's notes the only entry which could have formed the basis for such a remark is attributed not to Saunders but to Hyram Jackway, who told Kelley that "Hyram and his father owed Mr. Jaynes 150$" (p. 12).
51. Unpublished statement of Lorenzo Saunders, 1–3, 7–8, RLDS church archives.
52. See Anderson, 312.

Chapter 7

THE RECOLLECTIONS OF
LUCY MACK SMITH AND WILLIAM SMITH

ichard Anderson's final argument in his defense of Joseph Smith's New York reputation is that the recollections of Smith's own family provide the best refutation of the Hurlbut and Deming affidavits. Certainly the Smiths were in a better position to report accurately on young Joseph's activities and character than Hurlbut's or Deming's witnesses, but granting this does not mean that they necessarily did so. Indeed, from evidence to follow, the family was as intent on concealing certain facts as Hurlbut's and Deming's witnesses were to reveal them. The Smith family reminiscences, while valuable, cannot therefore be opposed to the testimony of more hostile witnesses simply on the grounds of their unsupported say-so.

An illustration of how the Smiths reacted to adverse criticism may be found in William Smith's recollection of the family's drinking habits. According to him, "I never knew my father Joseph Smith to be intoxicated or the worse for liquor, nor was my brother Joseph Smith in the habit of drinking spiritous liquors."[1] William's statement, made in 1875, was intended to contradict the many witnesses claiming to have seen Joseph Smith and his father drunk, but William only succeeded in proving himself either uniformed or deliberately untruthful. Besides the host of witnesses contradicting William's recollection, there also exist other evidences proving his statement less than candid. If his family was not "in the habit of drinking spiritous liquors," it is difficult to explain the entries in neighborhood grocer Lemual Durfee's account book recording the sale of numerous barrels of "cider liquor" to Joseph, Hyrum, and Samuel Smith during the years 1827–28.

Similarly, if Joseph Smith, Sr., was never "intoxicated or the worse for liquor," it is difficult to explain a remark he made on 9 December 1834, while giving a blessing to his son Hyrum. On that occasion the elder Smith said regarding himself, "Though he has been out of the way, through wine, thou hast never forsaken him nor laughed him to scorn."[2] William Smith was certainly in a position to report truthfully on this and other matters, but such apparently intentional misrepresentations prove him to be more concerned with defending his family's reputation than with writing authentic history.

Much the same may be said of the recollections of Lucy Mack Smith. According to one Mormon writer, her reminiscence of her famous son "reveals personal pride and much concern for the social status of her family,"[3] qualities which would hardly encourage her to report fully on such activities as money digging. Thus in explaining why Joseph Stowell hired her son in 1825, she says only that Stowell "came for Joseph on account of having heard that he possessed certain means, by which he could discern things invisible to the natural eye."[4] She does not explain what it was her son possessed which enabled him to see things otherwise invisible, nor does she specify what rumors prompted Stowell, a known money digger, to seek out the services of her son in locating a lost silver mine. Lucy does not provide these particulars because to do so would be admitting that her son possessed a seer stone in which he could see "wonders," a practice she condemns in others as "ridiculous."[5]

Lucy further tries to minimize her son's early reputation as a scryer by claiming that all the stories of his money digging are traceable to his brief employment by Stowell in Pennsylvania. But as previously noted, Smith himself confessed that he had dug for "lost property" prior to his employment by Stowell, and Martin Harris said that Smith dug for money in New York for some time after his return from Pennsylvania. Harris also reported that when Smith brought home the gold plates, "Mr. Stowel was at this time at old Mr. Smith's, digging for money," and related many stories told him by the diggers about the "strange sights" they had witnessed in their quest for buried treasures.[6] Lucy, however, says only that Stowell came to help the family with certain legal difficulties and mentions nothing about the money digging. Like her son Joseph, she admitted the charge of money digging but attempted to make it appear far less extensive than it evidently was.

In addition to Lucy Mack Smith's selective memory, the editors of her dictated reminiscences, Martha and Howard Coray, deleted from the published account such ambiguous statements as Lucy's denial that she and her family "stopt our labor and went at trying to win the faculty of Abrac, drawing magic circles, or sooth saying, to the neglect of all kinds of business. We never during our lives suffered one important interest to swallow up every other obligation."[7] The implication is that the family did engage in a bit of "sooth saying"—just not to the extent claimed by their neighbors. Lucy's editors, however, deleted the remark so as not to give credibility to the many stories linking the Smiths to the practice of magic.

These attempts by Lucy Mack Smith, William Smith, and the Corays to present the Smith family in the best possible light do not discredit their accounts. One expects some selectivity in autobiographies, even if in the end this is unnecessary. Lucy Smith could have admitted both her family's occult activities and their more "religious" pursuits, correctly maintaining that there is no necessary disharmony between the two. However, because many of her neighbors found the roles of money digger and prophet contradictory, Lucy apparently felt obligated to emphasize the latter role over the former.

William Smith responded in a similar way to criticisms about his family's drinking habits. The fact that his father had a drinking problem is unfortunate but ultimately irrelevant to the religious claims of Joseph Smith, just as Smith's own occasional indulgences do not prove his visions mere subjective fantasies. However, rather than present to the world a photograph from life, Lucy and William chose to offer an idealized portrait of their family—a task which has since been assumed by Hugh Nibley, Richard Anderson, and others.

NOTES

1. Notes written on *Chambers' Miscellany*, 6, in Richard L. Anderson, "Joseph Smith's New York Reputation Reappraised," *Brigham Young University Studies* 10 (Spring 1970): 314. Born in 1811, William was in his teens during much of the 1820s.
2. Durfee's account book is in the Palmyra King's Daughters Free Library, Inc. Joseph Smith Sr.'s remark occurred as part of a patriarchal blessing to Hyrum Smith; original in the Hyrum Smith papers, archives, historical department, Church of Jesus Christ of Latter-day Saints, Salt Lake City, Utah. Durfee's account book lends some support to Martin Harris's charge, made in 1834, "that Joseph drank too much liquor when he was

translating the Book of Mormon." Later, when called to account for the remark, Harris amended his statement to mean "this thing occurred previous to the translating of the book." *Times and Seasons* 6 (15 Aug. 1845): 992.

3. Donna Hill, *Joseph Smith: The First Mormon* (Garden City, NY: Doubleday, 1977), 32.

4. Lucy Mack Smith, *Biographical Sketches* . . . (Liverpool: S. W. Richards, 1853), 91–92.

5. Lucy Mack Smith, 102.

6. *Tiffany's Monthly* 5 (Aug. 1859): 165. Richard Anderson attempts to dismiss Harris's remarks by claiming "contamination" from the reporter, Joel Tiffany, who may have read Eber D. Howe's *Mormonism Unvailed* before interviewing Harris. Such a conjecture is unlikely for the simple reason that much of the information contained in Tiffany's report is not found in Howe. This includes most of the money-digging and scrying incidents, which while compatible with Hurlbut's evidence, clearly come from another source. Nor is there much mystery about who this other source was. Tiffany stated that it was Martin Harris who wanted the account written up and that the narration was taken not from Tiffany's memory but "from the lips of Martin Harris, and read . . . to him after it was written, that we might be certain of giving his statement to the world" (p. 163). Harris, it should be noted, at no time denied the accuracy of Tiffany's report.

7. D. Michael Quinn, *Early Mormonism and the Magic World View* (Salt Lake City: Signature Books, 1987), 54–55.

Chapter 8

CONCLUSION

Four conclusions emerge from the foregoing reexamination of Joseph Smith's New York reputation. First, I can find no evidence that the primary source affidavits and other documents collected by Philastus Hurlbut, Eber D. Howe, and Arthur B. Deming are other than what they purport to be. The men and women whose names they bear either wrote them or authorized them to be written. Ghost-writing may have colored some of the testimony, but there is no evidence that the vast majority of testators did not write or dictate their own statements or share the attitudes attributed to them.

Second, every contemporary attempt to impugn these accounts failed. Book of Mormon witness Martin Harris's effort to prove Isaac Hale's letter a forgery was contradicted by Hale himself. The attempts by Lucy Mack Smith and William Smith to exonerate the Smith family of certain charges were undone by the more candid admissions of friends or other family members. And RLDS apostle William Kelley's report, designed to discredit Joseph

Smith's debunkers, was itself discredited by many of those contacted by Kelley. The fact that these efforts resulted in impeaching not a single witness who testified against Smith, though many of these same witnesses were still alive and willing to repeat their testimony, supports the conclusion that the statements collected by Hurlbut and Deming can be relied on as accurate reflections of their signers' views.

Third, with the possible exception of Peter Ingersoll, there is no evidence that the witnesses contacted by Hurlbut in 1833-34 and Deming in 1888 perjured themselves by knowingly swearing to a lie. In fact, existing evidence goes far to substantiate the recorded stories. The harmony of the accounts, the fact that they were collected by different people at different times and places, and the sometimes impressive confirmations supplied by independent witnesses or documents never intended for public consumption discredit the argument that the work of Hurlbut and Deming contains nothing but "trumped-up evidence."

Fourth, there is no evidence that the majority of witnesses indulged in malicious defamation by repeating groundless rumors. Many based their descriptions on close association with the Joseph Smith, Sr., family. They did not always distinguish hearsay from observation, fact from inference, but they generally state whether or not the source of the information is firsthand, and several witnesses provided enough information to demonstrate that much of what was previously thought to be popular rumor about the Smiths was not wholly groundless.

Having survived the determined criticism of Mormon scholars Hugh Nibley and Richard L. Anderson, the Hurlbut-Deming affidavits must be granted permanent status as primary documents relating to Joseph Smith's early life and the origins of Mormonism. In using the reminiscences, however, several measures of reliability should be followed. For one, preference should be given to witnesses speaking from personal, direct knowledge, not hearsay or obvious neighborhood gossip. The recitals of Isaac Butts, Joseph Capron, Willard Chase, Isaac Hale, Abigail Harris, Henry Harris, W. R. Hine, and William Stafford are primary examples of witnesses having firsthand experience with members of the Smith family and Martin Harris. The general Manchester and Palmyra, New York, affidavits are less useful in this regard.

For another, two or more accounts relating specific incidents in essentially identical detail are probably more reliable than recitals of events relying on one source only. Abigail Harris and Lucy Harris left separate but similar accounts of Martin Harris's initial financial interest in the Book of Mormon. Joseph Smith's promise that the plates from which he translated the Book of Mormon were to be placed on public display as evidence of the truth of the book was remembered by Nathaniel Lewis, Joshua M'Kune, and Alva Hale, among others. Sophia Lewis and Joshua M'Kune also recalled Joseph Smith's statement that his first born son would be able to open and read the Book of Mormon plates. And the unanimity of individual testimony regarding the consumption of alcohol and treasure hunting is striking.

Finally, accounts by non-Mormons containing information that can be substantiated by Mormon witnesses, such as Joseph Smith, Lucy Mack Smith, Martin Harris, Joseph Knight, Oliver Cowdery, or David Whitmer, may also be accurate in their uncorroborated claims.

In general terms, the Hurlbut, Howe, Deming, and Kelley testimonials paint a portrait of a young frontiersman and his family struggling to eke out a minimal existence in western New York, facing the discouraging realities of life on the margins of society. Intelligent and quick-witted, if not always a hard worker, Joseph Smith, Jr., had been brought up by parents who believed in angels, evil spirits, and ghosts; in buried treasures that slipped into the earth if the proper rituals were not performed to exhume them; in divining rods and seer stones; in dreams and visions; and that despite their indigent status, their's was a family chosen by God for a worthy purpose.

Following the death of their eldest son Alvin, on whom the family had placed their dreams, Joseph Jr. seems to have assumed the role of favored son. Whether hunting for buried treasure or the ancient record of a lost civilization, neither Joseph nor his family saw any conflict between the secular pressures of earning a living, even by so esoteric a means as money digging, and a religious quest for spiritual fulfillment. If they could accomplish one goal by pursuing the other, so much the better.

Nondescript and of little consequence until he started attracting others to his peculiar blend of biblical Christianity, frontier folk belief, popular culture, and personal experience, Joseph Smith was an enigma to his incredulous New York neighbors. For them, he would always remain a superstitious adolescent dreamer and his success as a prophet a riddle for which there was no answer.

Appendix

THE AFFIDAVITS, STATEMENTS, AND INTERVIEWS

[Note: The following documents are reproduced exactly as they appear in the original published or unpublished sources, with the exception of arranging them either alphabetically or chronologically. As with any endeavor of this kind, however, it is possible that some errors of transcription may exist.]

A. THE PHILASTUS HURLBUT/EBER D. HOWE AFFIDAVITS, FROM:

E. D. HOWE, *MORMONISM UNVAILED [SIC]: OR,*

A FAITHFUL ACCOUNT OF THAT SINGULAR IMPOSITION

AND DELUSION, FROM ITS RISE TO THE PRESENT TIME.

WITH SKETCHES OF THE CHARACTERS OF ITS PROPAGATORS,

AND A FULL DETAIL OF THE MANNER IN WHICH THE FAMOUS

GOLD BIBLE WAS BROUGHT BEFORE THE WORLD,

TO WHICH ARE ADDED, INQUIRIES INTO THE PROBABILITY

THAT THE HISTORICAL PART OF THE SAID BIBLE WAS WRITTEN

BY ONE SOLOMON SPAULDING, MORE THAN TWENTY YEARS

AGO, AND BY HIM INTENDED TO HAVE BEEN PUBLISHED AS A

ROMANCE. (PAINESVILLE, OHIO: PRINTED AND PUBLISHED

BY THE AUTHOR, 1834), PAGES 232–69

I. INDIVIDUAL AFFIDAVITS (ARRANGED ALPHABETICALLY ACCORDING TO SURNAME OF TESTATOR):

1. Joseph Capron

Manchester, Ontario County, Nov. 8th, 1833.

I, Joseph Capron, became acquainted with Joseph Smith, Sen. in the year of our Lord, 1827. They have, since then, been really a peculiar people—fond of the foolish and the marvelous—at one time addicted to vice and the grossest immoralities—at another time making the highest pretensions to piety and holy intercourse with Almighty God. The family of Smiths held Joseph Jr. in high estimation on account of some supernatural power, which he was supposed to possess. This power he pretended to have received through the medium of a stone of peculiar quality. The stone was placed in a hat, in such a manner as to exclude all light, except that which emanated from the stone itself. This light of the stone, he pretended, enabled him to see any thing he wished. Accordingly he discovered ghosts, infernal spirits, mountains of gold and silver, and many other invaluable treasures deposited in the earth. He would often tell his neighbors of his wonderful discoveries, and urge them to embark in the money digging business. Luxury and wealth were to be given to all who would adhere to his counsel. A gang was soon assembled. Some of them were influenced by curiosity, others were sanguine in their expectations of immediate gain. I will mention one circumstance, by which the uninitiated may know how the company dug for treasures. The sapient Joseph discovered, north west of my house, a chest of gold watches; but, as they were in the possession of the evil spirit, it required skill and stratagem to obtain them. Accordingly, orders were given to stick a parcel of large stakes in the ground, several rods around, in a circular form. This was to be done directly over the spot where the treasures were deposited. A messenger was then sent to Palmyra to procure a polished sword: after which, Samuel F. Lawrence, with a drawn sword in his hand, marched around to guard any assault which his Satanic majesty might be disposed to make. Meantime, the rest of the company were busily employed in digging for the watches. They worked as usual till quite exhausted. But, in spite of their brave defender, Lawrence, and their bulwark of stakes, the devil came off victorious, and carried away the watches. I might mention numerous schemes by which this young visionary and impostor had recourse to for the purpose of obtaining a livelihood. He, and indeed the whole of the family of Smiths, were notorious for indolence, foolery and falsehood. Their great object appeared to be, to live without work. While they were digging for money, they were daily harrassed by the demands of creditors, which they never were able to pay. At length, Joseph pretended to find the Gold plates. This scheme, he believed, would relieve the family from all pecuniary embarrassment. His father told me, that when the book was published, they would be enabled, from the profits of the work, to carry into successful operation the money digging business. He gave me no intimation, at that time that the book was to be of a religious character, or that it had any thing to do with revelation. He declared it to be a speculation, and said he, "when it is completed, my family will be placed *on a level* above the generality of mankind"!!

JOSEPH CAPRON.

2. Parley Chase

Manchester, December 2d, 1833.

I was acquainted with the family of Joseph Smith, Sen., both before and since they became Mormons, and feel free to state that not one of the male members of the Smith family were entitled to any credit, whatsoever. They were lazy, intemperate and worthless men, very much addicted to lying. In this they freqently boasted of their skill. Digging for money was their principal employment. In regard to their Gold Bible speculation, they scarcely ever told two stories alike. The Mormon Bible is said to be a revelation from God, through Joseph Smith Jr., his Prophet, and this same Joseph Smith Jr. to my knowledge, bore the reputation among his neighbors of being a liar. The foregoing statement can be corroborated by all his former neighbors.

PARLEY CHASE.

3. Willard Chase

Manchester, Ontario Co. N.Y. 1833.

I became acquainted with the Smith family, known as the authors of the Mormon Bible, in the year 1820. At that time, they were engaged in the money digging business, which they followed until the latter part of the season of 1827. In the year 1822, I was engaged in digging a well. I employed Alvin and Joseph Smith to assist me; the latter of whom is now known as the Mormon prophet. After digging about twenty feet below the surface of the earth, we discovered a singularly appearing stone, which excited my curiosity. I brought it to the top of the well, and as we were examining it, Joseph put it into his hat, and then his face into the top of his hat. It has been said by Smith, that *he* brought the stone from the well; but this is false. There was no one in the well but myself. The next morning he came to me, and wished to obtain the stone, alledging that he could see in it; but I told him I did not wish to part with it on account of its being a curiosity, but would lend it. After obtaining the stone, he began to publish abroad what wonders he could discover by looking in it, and made so much disturbance among the credulous part of community, that I ordered the stone to be returned to me again. He had it in his possession about two years. —I believe, some time in 1825, Hiram Smith (brother of Joseph Smith) came to me, and wished to borrow the same stone, alledging that they wanted to accomplish some business of importance, which could not very well be done without the aid of the stone. I told him it was of no particular worth to me, but merely wished to keep it as a curiosity, and if he would pledge me his word and honor, that I should have it when called for, he might take it; which he did and took the stone. I thought I could rely on his word at this time, as he had made a profession of religion. But in this I was disappointed, for he disregarded both his word and honor.

In the fall of 1826, a friend called upon me and wished to see that stone, about which so much had been said; and I told him if he would go with me to Smith's, (a distance of about half a mile) he might see it. But to my surprize, on going to Smith's, and asking him for the stone, he said, "you cannot have it;" I told him it belonged to me, repeated to him the promise he made me, at the time of obtaining the stone: upon which he faced me with a malignant look and said, "I don't care who in the Devil it belongs to, *you* shall not have it."

In the month of June, 1827, Joseph Smith, Sen., related to me the following story: "That some years ago, a spirit had appeared to Joseph his son, in a vision, and informed him that in a certain place there was a record on plates of gold, and that he was the person that must obtain them, and this he must do in the following manner: On the 22d of September, he must repair to the place where was deposited this manuscript, dressed in black clothes, and riding a black horse with a switch tail, and demand the book in a certain name, and after obtaining it, he must go directly away, and neither lay it down nor look behind him. They accordingly fitted out Joseph with a suit of black clothes and borrowed a black horse. He repaired to the place of deposit and demanded the book, which was in a stone box, unsealed, and so near the top of the ground that he could see one end of it, and raising it up, took out the book of gold; but fearing some one might discover where he got it, he laid it down to place back the top stone, as he found it; and turning round, to his surprise there was no book in sight. He again opened the box, and in it saw the book, and attempted to take it out, but was hindered. He saw in the box something like a toad, which soon assumed the appearance of a man, and struck him on the side of his head. — Not being discouraged at trifles, he again stooped down and strove to take the book, when the spirit struck him again, and knocked him three or four rods, and hurt him prodigiously. After recovering from his fright, he enquired why he could not obtain the plates; to which the spirit made reply, because you have not obeyed your orders. He then enquired when he *could* have them, and was answered thus: come one year from this day, and bring with you your oldest brother, and you shall have them. This spirit, he said was the spirit of the prophet who wrote this book, and who was sent to Joseph Smith, to make known these things to him. Before the expiration of the year, his oldest brother died; which the old man said was an *accidental providence!*

Joseph went one year from that day, to demand the book, and the spirit enquired for his brother, and he said that he was dead. The spirit then commanded him to come again, in just one year, and bring a man with him. On asking who might be the man, he was answered that he would know him when he saw him.

Joseph believed that one Samuel T. Lawrence was the man alluded to by the spirit, and went with him to a singular looking hill, in Manchester, and shewed him where the treasure was. Lawrence asked him if he had ever discovered any thing with the plates of gold; he said no: he then asked him to look in his stone, to see if there was any thing with them. He looked, and said there was nothing; he told him to look again, and see if there was not a large pair of specks with the plates; he looked and soon saw a pair of spectacles, the same with which Joseph says he translated the Book of Mormon. Lawrence told him it would not be prudent to let these plates be seen for about two years, as it would make a great disturbance in the neighborhood. Not long after this, Joseph altered his mind, and said L. was not the right man, nor had he told him the right place. About this time he went to Harmony in Pennsylvania, and formed an acquaintance with a young lady, by the name of Emma Hale, whom he wished to marry. —In the fall of 1826, he wanted to go to Pennsylvania to be married; but being destitute of means, he now set his wits to work, how he should raise money, and get recommendations, to procure the fair one of his choice. He went to Lawrence with the following story, as related to me by Lawrence himself. That he had discovered in Pennsylvania, on the bank of the Susquehannah River, a very rich mine of silver, and if he would go there with him, he might have a share in the profits; that it was near high water mark and that they could load it into boats and take it down the river to Philadelphia, to market. Lawrence then asked Joseph if he was not deceiving him; no, said he, for I have been there and seen it with my own eyes, and if you do not find it so when we get there, I will bind myself to be your servant for three years. By these grave and fair promises Lawrence was induced to believe something in it, and agreed to go with him. L. soon found that Joseph was out of money, and had to bear his expenses on the way. When they got to Pennsylvania, Joseph wanted L. to recommend him to Miss H., which he did, although he was asked to do it; but could not well get rid of it as he was in his company. L. then wished to see the silver mine, and he and Joseph went to the river, and made search, but found nothing. Thus, Lawrence had his trouble for his pains, and returned home lighter than he went, while Joseph had got his expenses borne, and a recommendation to his girl.

Joseph's next move was to get married; the girl's parents being opposed to the match: as they happened to be from home, he took advantage of the opportunity, and went off with her and was married.

Now, being still destitute of money, he set his wits at work, how he should get back to Manchester, his place of residence; he hit upon the following plan, which succeeded very well. He went to an honest old Dutchman, by the name of Stowel, and told him that he had discovered on the bank of Black River, in the village of Watertown, Jefferson County, N.Y. a cave, in which he had found a bar of gold, as big as his leg, and about three or four feet long. −That he could not get it out alone, on account of its being fast at one end; and if he would move him to Manchester, N.Y. they would go together, and take a chisel and mallet, and get it, and Stowel should share the prize with him. Stowel moved him.

A short time after their arrival at Manchester, Stowel reminded Joseph of his promise; but he calmly replied, that he would not go, because his wife was now among strangers, and would be very lonesome if he went away. Mr. Stowel was then obliged to return without any gold, and with less money than he came.

In the fore part of September, (I believe,) 1827, the Prophet requested me to make him a chest, informing me that he designed to move back to Pennsylvania, and expecting soon to get his gold book, he wanted a chest to lock it up, giving me to understand at the same time, that if I would make the chest he would give me a share in the book. I told him my business was such that I could not make it: but if he would bring the book to me, I would lock it up for him. He said that would not do, as he was commanded to keep it two years, without letting it come to the eye of any one but himself. This commandment, however, he did not keep, for in less than two years, twelve men said they had seen it. I told him to get it and convince me of its existence, and I would make him a chest; but he said, that would not do, as he must have a chest to lock the book in, as soon as he took it out of the ground. I saw him a few days after, when he told me that I must make the chest. I told him plainly that I could not, upon which he told me that I could have no share in the book.

A few weeks after this conversation, he came to my house, and related the following story: That on the 22d of September, he arose early in the morning, and took a one horse wagon, of some one that had stayed over night at their house, without leave or license; and, together with his wife, repaired to the hill which contained the book. He left his wife in the wagon, by the road, and went alone to the hill, a distance of thirty or forty rods from the road; he said he then took the book out of the ground and hid it in a tree top, and returned home. He then went to the town of Macedon to work. After about ten days, it having been suggested that some one had got his book, his wife went after him; he hired a horse, and went home in the afternoon, staid long enough to drink one cup of tea, and then went for his book, found it safe, took off his frock, wrapt it round it, put it under his arm and run all the way home, a distance of about two miles. He said he should think it would weigh sixty pounds, and was sure it would weigh forty. On his return home, he said he was attacked by two men in the woods, and knocked them both down and made his escape, arrived safe and secured his treasure. —He then observed that if it had not been for that stone, (which he acknowledged belonged to me,) he would not have obtained the book. A few days afterwards, he told one of my neighbors that he had not got any such book, nor never had such an one; but that he had told the story to deceive the d—-d fool, (meaning me,) to get him to make a chest. His neighbors having become disgusted with his foolish stories, he determined to go back to Pennsylvania, to avoid what he called persecution. His wits were now put to the task to contrive how he should get money to bear his expenses. He met one day in the streets of Palmyra, a rich man, whose name was Martin Harris, and addressed him thus; "I have a commandment from God to ask the first man I meet in the street to give me fifty dollars, to assist me in doing the work of the Lord by translating the Golden Bible." Martin being naturally a credulous man, hands Joseph the money. In the Spring 1829, Harris went to Pennsylvania, and on his return to Palmyra, reported that the Prophet's wife, in the month of June following would be delivered of a male child that would be able when two years old to translate the Gold Bible. Then, said he, you will see Joseph Smith, Jr. walking through the streets of Palmyra, with a Gold Bible under his arm, and having a gold breast-plate on, and a gold sword hanging by his side. This, however, by the by, proved false.

In April, 1830, I again asked Hiram for the stone which he had borrowed of me; he told me I should not have it, for Joseph made use of it in translating his Bible. I reminded him of his promise, and that he had pledged his honor to return it; but he gave me the lie, saying the stone was not mine nor never was. Harris at the same time flew in a rage, took me by the collar and said I was a liar, and he could prove it by twelve witnesses. After I had extricated myself from him, Hiram, in a rage shook his fist at me, and abused me in a most scandalous manner. Thus I might proceed in describing the character of these High Priests, by relating one transaction after another, which would all tend to set them in the same light in which they were regarded by their neighbors, viz: as a pest to society. I have regarded Joseph Smith Jr. from the time I first became acquainted with him until he left this part of the country, as a man whose word could not be depended upon. —Hiram's character was but very little better. What I have said respecting the characters of these men, will apply to the whole family. What I have stated relative to the characters of these individuals, thus far, is wholly true. After they became thorough Mormons, their conduct was more disgraceful than before. They did not hesitate to abuse any man, no matter how fair his character, provided he did not embrace their creed. Their tongues were continually employed in spreading scandal and abuse. Although they left this part of the country without paying their just debts, yet their creditors were glad to have them do so, rather than to have them stay, disturbing the neighborhood.

Signed,   WILLARD CHASE.

On the 11th December, 1833, the said Willard Chase appeared before me, and made oath that the foregoing statement to which he has subscribed his name, is true, according to his best recollection and belief.

FRED'K. SMITH,
Justice of the Peace of Wayne County.

4. Isaac Hale

Harmony, Pa. March 20th, 1834.

I first became acquainted with Joseph Smith, Jr. in November, 1825. He was at that time in the employ of a set of men who were called "money diggers;" and his occupation was that of seeing, or pretending to see by means of a stone placed in his hat, and his hat closed over his face. In this way he pretended to discover minerals and hidden treasure. His appearance at this time, was that of a careless young man—not very well educated, and very saucy and insolent to his father. Smith, and his father, with several other 'money-diggers' boarded at my house while they were employed in digging for a mine that they supposed had been opened and worked by the Spaniards, many years since. Young Smith gave the 'money-diggers' great encouragement, at first, but when they had arrived in digging, to near the place where he had stated an immense treasure would be found—he said the enchantment was so powerful that he could not see. They then became discouraged, and soon after dispersed. This took place about the 17th of November, 1825; and one of the company gave me his note for $12.68 for his board, which is still unpaid.

After these occurrences, young Smith made several visits at my house, and at length asked my consent to his marrying my daughter Emma. This I refused, and gave my reasons for so doing; some of which were, that he was a stranger, and followed a business that I could not approve; he then left the place. Not long after this, he returned, and while I was absent from home, carried off my daughter, into the state of New York, where they were married without my approbation or consent. After they had arrived at Palmyra N.Y., Emma wrote to me enquiring whether she could take her property, consisting of clothing, furniture, cows, &c. I replied that her property was safe, and at her disposal. In a short time they returned, bringing with them a Peter Ingersol, and subsequently came to the conclusion that they would move out, and reside upon a place near my residence.

Smith stated to me, that he had given up what he called "glass-looking," and that he expected to work hard for a living, and was willing to do so. He also made arrangements with my son Alva Hale, to go to Palmyra, and move his (Smith's) furniture &c. to this place. He then returned to Palmyra, and soon after, Alva, agreeable to the arrangement, went up and returned with Smith and his family. Soon after this, I was informed they had brought a wonderful book of Plates down with them. I was shown a box in which it is said they were contained, which had to all appearances, been used as a glass box of the common window glass. I was allowed to feel the weight of the box, and they gave me to understand, that the book of plates was then in the box—into which, however, I was not allowed to look.

I inquired of Joseph Smith Jr., who was to be the first who would be allowed to see the Book of Plates? He said it was a young child. After this, I became dissatisfied, and informed him that if there was any thing in my house of that description, which I could not be allowed to see, he must take it away; if he did not, I was determined to see it. After that, the Plates were said to be hid in the woods.

About this time, Martin Harris made his appearance upon the stage; and Smith began to interpret the characters or hieroglyphics which he said were engraven upon the plates, while Harris wrote down the interpretation. It was said, that Harris wrote down one hundred and sixteen pages, and lost them. Soon after this happened, Martin Harris informed me that he must have a *greater witness*, and said that he had talked with Joseph about it—Joseph informed him that he could not, or durst not show him the plates, but that he (Joseph) would go into the woods where the Book of Plates was, and that after he came back, Harris should follow his track in the snow, and find the Book, and examine it for himself. Harris informed me afterwards, that he followed Smith's directions, and could not find the Plates, and was still dissatisfied.

The next day after this happened, I went to the house where Joseph Smith Jr., lived, and where he and Harris were engaged in their translation of the Book. Each of them had a written piece of paper which they were comparing, and some of the words were *"my servant seeketh a greater witness, but no greater witness can be given him."* There was also something said about *"three that were to see the thing"*—meaning I supposed, the Book of Plates, and that *"if the three did not go exactly according to the orders, the thing would be taken from them."* I enquired whose words they were, and was informed by Joseph or Emma, (I rather think it was the former) that they were the words of Jesus Christ. I told them, that I considered the whole of it a delusion, and advised them to abandon it. The manner in which he pretended to read and interpret, was the same as when he looked for the money-diggers, with the stone in his hat, and his hat over his face, while the Book of Plates were at the same time hid in the woods!

After this, Martin Harris went away, and Oliver Cowdery came and wrote for Smith, while he interpreted as above described. This is the same Oliver Cowdery, whose name may be found in the Book of Mormon. Cowdery continued a scribe

for Smith until the Book of Mormon was completed as I supposed and understood.

Joseph Smith Jr. resided near me for some time after
this, and I had a good opportunity of becoming acquainted with
him, and somewhat acquainted with his associates, and I conscientiously believe from the facts I have detailed, and from many
other circumstances, which I do not deem it necessary to relate,
that the whole "Book of Mormon" (so called) is a silly fabrication
of falsehood and wickedness, got up for speculation, and with a
design to dupe the credulous and unwary—and in order that its
fabricators may live upon the spoils of those who swallow the
deception.

ISAAC HALE.

Affirmed to and subscribed before me, March 20th, 1834.

CHARLES DIMON, *J. Peace.*
State of Pennsylvania, Susquehana County, ss.

We, the subscribers, associate Judges of the Court of
Common Pleas, in and for said county, do certify that we have
been many years personally acquainted with Isaac Hale, of Harmony township in this county, who has attested the foregoing
statement; and that he is a man of excellent moral character, and
of undoubted veracity. Witness our hands.

WILLIAM THOMPSON.
DAVIS DIMOCK.

5. Abigail Harris

Palmyra, Wayne Co. N.Y. 11th mo. 28th, 1833.

In the early part of the winter in 1828, I made a visit
to Martin Harris' and was joined in company by Jos. Smith, sen.
and his wife. The Gold Bible business, so called, was the topic of
conversation, to which I paid particular attention, that I might
learn the truth of the whole matter. —They told me that the re-

port that Joseph, jun. had found golden plates, was true, and that he was in Harmony, Pa. translating them—that such plates were in existence, and that Joseph, jun. was to obtain them, was revealed to him by the spirit of one of the Saints that was on this continent, previous to its being discovered by Columbus. Old Mrs. Smith observed that she thought he must be a Quaker, as he was dressed very plain. They said that the plates he then had in possession were but an introduction to the Gold Bible—that all of them upon which the bible was written, were so heavy that it would take four stout men to load them into a cart—that Joseph had also discovered by looking through his stone, the vessel in which the gold was melted from which the plates were made, and also the machine with which they were rolled; he also discovered in the bottom of the vessel three balls of gold, each as large as his fist. The old lady said also, that after the book was translated, the plates were to be publicly exhibited—admitance 25 cents. She calculated it would bring in annually an enormous sum of money—that money would then be very plenty, and the book would also sell for a great price, as it was something entirely new—that they had been commanded to obtain all the money they could borrow for present necessity, and to repay with gold. The remainder was to be kept in store for the benefit of their family and children. This and the like conversation detained me until about 11 o'clock. Early the next morning, the mystery of the Spirit being like myself (one of the order called Friends) was reveal by the following circumstance: The old lady took me into another room, and after closing the door, she said, "have you four or five dollars in money that you can lend until our business is brought to a close? the spirit has said you shall receive four fold." I told her that when I gave, I did it not expecting to receive again—as for money I had none to lend. I then asked her what her particular want of money was; to which she replied, "Joseph wants to take the stage and come home from Pennsylvania to see what we are all about." To which I replied, he might look in his stone and save his time and money. The old lady seemed confused, and left the room, and thus ended the visit.

In the second month following, Martin Harris and his

wife were at my house. In conversation about Mormonites, she observed, that she wished her husband would quit them, as she believed it was all false and delusion. To which I head Mr. Harris reply: *"What if it is a lie; if you will let me alone I will make money out of it!"* I was both an eye and an ear witness of what has been stated above, which is now fresh in my memory, and I give it to the world for the good of mankind. I speak the truth and lie not, God bearing me witness.

ABIGAIL HARRIS

6. Henry Harris

I, Henry Harris, do state that I became acquainted with the family of Joseph Smith, Sen. about the year 1820, in the town of Manchester, N. York. They were a family that labored very little—the chief they did, was to dig for money. Joseph Smith, Jr. the pretended Prophet, used to pretend to tell fortunes; he had a stone which he used to put in his hat, by means of which he professed to tell people's fortunes.

Joseph Smith, Jr. Martin Harris and others, used to meet together in private, a while before the gold plates were found, and were familiarly known by the name of the "Gold Bible Company." They were regarded by the community in which they lived, as a lying and indolent set of men and no confidence could be placed in them.

The character of Joseph Smith, Jr. for truth and veracity was such, that I would not believe him under oath. I was once on a jury before a Justice's Court and the Jury could not, and did not, believe his testimony to be true. After he pretended to have found the gold plates, I had a conversation with him, and asked him where he found them and how he come to know where they were. He said he had a revelation from God that told him they were hid in a certain hill and he looked in his stone and saw them in the place of deposit; that an angel appeared, and told him he could not get the plates until he was married, and that when he saw the woman that was to be his wife, he should know her, and she would know him. He then went to Pennsylvania, got his wife, and they both went together and got the gold plates—he said it was revealed to him, that no one must see the plates but himself and wife.

I then asked him what letters were engraved on them, he said italic letters written in an unknown language, and that he had copied some of the words and sent them to Dr. Mitchell and Professor Anthon of New York. By looking on the plates he said he could not understand the words, but it was made known to him that he was the person that must translate them, and on looking through the stone was enabled to translate.

After the Book was published, I frequently bantered him for a copy. He asked fourteen shillings a piece for them; I told him I would not give so much; he told me had had a revelation that they must be sold at that price.

Sometime afterwards I talked with Martin Harris about buying one of the Books and he told me they had had a new revelation, that they might be sold at ten shillings a piece.

State of Ohio, Cuyahoga County, ss:

Personally appeared before me, Henry Harris, and made oath in due form of law, that the foregoing statements subscribed by him are true.

JONATHAN LAPHAM,
Justice of the Peace.

7. Lucy Harris

Palmyra, Nov. 29, 1833.

Being called upon to give a statement to the world of what I know respecting the Gold Bible speculation, and also of the conduct of Martin Harris, my husband, who is a leading character among the Mormons, I do it free from prejudice, realizing that I must give an account at the bar of God for what I say. Martin Harris was once industrious attentive to his domestic concerns, and thought to be worth about ten thousand dollars. He is naturally quick in his temper and his mad-fits frequently abuses all who may dare to oppose him in his wishes. However strange it may seem, I have been a great sufferer by his unreasonable conduct. At different times while I lived with him, he has whipped, kicked, and turned me out of the house. About a year previous to the report being raised that Smith had found gold plates, he became very intimate with the Smith family, and said he believed Joseph could see in his stone any thing he wished. After this he apparently became very sanguine in his belief, and frequently said he would have no one in his house that did not believe in Mormonism; and because I would not give credit to the report he made about the gold plates, he became more austere towards me. In one of his fits of rage he struck me with the but end of a whip, which I think had been used for driving oxen, and was about the size of my thumb, and three or four feet long. He beat me on the head four or five times, and the next day turned me out of doors twice, and beat me in a shameful manner. —The next day I went to the town of Marion, and while there my flesh was black and blue in many places. His main complaint against me was, that I was always trying to hinder his making money.

When he found out that I was going to Mr. Putnam's, in Marion, he said he was going too, but they had sent for him to pay them a visit. On arriving at Mr. Putnam's, I asked them if they had sent for Mr. Harris; they replied, they knew nothing about it; he, however, came in the evening. Mrs. Putnam told him never to strike or abuse me any more; he then denied ever striking me; she was however convinced that he lied, as the marks of his beating me were plain to be seen, and remained more than two weeks. Whether the Mormon religion be true or false, I leave the world to judge, for its effects upon Martin Harris have been to make him more cross, turbulent and abusive to me. His whole object was to make money by it. I will give one circumstance in proof of it. One day, while at Peter Harris' house, I told him he had better leave the company of the Smiths, as their religion was false; to which he replied, if you would let me alone, I could make money by it.

It is in vain for the Mormons to deny these facts; for

they are all well known to most of his former neighbors. The man has now become rather an object of pity; he has spent most of his property, and lost the confidence of his former friends. If he had labored as hard on his farm as he has to make Mormons, he might now be one of the wealthiest farmers in the country. He now spends his time in travelling through the country spreading the delusion of Mormonism, and has no regard whatever for his family.

With regard to Mr. Harris' being intimate with Mrs. Haggard, as has been reported, it is but justice to myself to state what facts have come within my own observation, to show whether I had any grounds for jealousy or not. Mr. Harris was very intimate with this family, for some time previous to their going to Ohio. They lived a while in a house which he had built for their accommodation, and here he spent the most of his leisure hours; and made her presents of articles from the store and house. He carried these presents in a private manner, and frequently when he went there, he would pretend to be going to some of the neighbors, on an errand, or to be going into the fields. — After getting out of sight of the house, he would steer a straight course for Haggard's house, especially if Haggard was from home. At times when Haggard was from home, he would go there in the manner above described, and stay till twelve or one o'clok at night, and sometimes until day light.

If his intentions were evil, the Lord will judge him accordingly, but if good, he did not mean to let his left hand know what his right hand did. The above statement of facts, I affirm to be true.

LUCY HARRIS

8. Peter Ingersoll

Palmyra, Wayne Co. N.Y. Dec. 2d, 1833.
I, Peter Ingersoll, first became acquainted with the family of Jopesh Smith, Sen. in the year of our Lord, 1822. —I lived in the neighborhood of said family, until about 1830; during which time the following facts came under my observation.

The general employment of the family, was digging for money. I had frequent invitations to join the company, but always declined being one of their number. They used various arguments to induce me to accept of their invitations. I was once ploughing near the house of Joseph Smith, Sen. about noon, he requested me to walk with him a short distance from his house, for the purpose of seeing whether a mineral rod would work in my hand, saying at the same time he was confident it would. As my oxen were eating, and being myself at leisure, I accepted the invitation. —When we arrived near the place at which he thought there was money, he cut a small witch hazle bush and gave me direction how to hold it. He then went off some rods, and told me to say to the rod, "work to the money," which I did, in an audible voice. He rebuked me severely for speaking it loud, and said it must be spoken in a whisper. This was rare sport for me. While the old man was standing off some rods, throwing himself into various shapes, I told him the rod did not work. He seemed much surprised at this, and said he thought he saw it move in my hand. It was now time for me to return to my labor. On my return, I picked up a small stone and was carelessly tossing it from one hand to the other. Said he, (looking very earnestly) what are you going to do with that stone? Throw it at the birds, I replied. No, said the old man, it is of great worth; and upon this I gave it to him. Now, says he, if you only knew the value there is back of my house (and pointing to a place near)—*there*, exclaimed he, is one chest of gold and another of silver. He then put the stone which I had given him, into his hat, and stooping forward, he bowed and made sundry maneuvers, quite similar to those of a stool pigeon. At length he took down his hat, and being very much exhausted, said, in a faint voice, "if you knew what I had seen, you would believe." To see the old man thus try to impose upon me, I confess, rather had a tendency to excite contempt than pity. Yet I thought it best to conceal my feelings, preferring to appear the dupe of my credulity, than to expose myself to his resentment. His son Alvin then went through with the same performance, which was equally disgusting.

Another time, the said Joseph, Sen. told me that the

best time for digging money, was, in the heat of summer, when the heat of the sun caused the chests of money to rise near the top of the ground. You notice, said he, the large stones on the top of the ground—we call them rocks, and they truly appear so, but they are, in fact, most of them chests of money raised by the heat of the sun.

At another time, he told me that the ancient inhabitants of this country used camels instead of horses. For proof of this fact, he stated that in a certain hill on the farm of Mr. Cuyler, there was a cave containing an immense value of gold and silver, stands of arms, also, a saddle for a camel, hanging on a peg at one side of the cave. I asked him, of what kind of wood the peg was. He could not tell, but said it had become similar to stone or iron.

The old man at last laid a plan which he thought would accomplish his design. His cows and mine had been gone for some time, and were not to be found, notwithstanding our diligent search for them. Day after day was spent in fruitless search, until at length he proposed to find them by his art of divination. So he took his stand near the corner of his house, with a small stick in his hand, and made several strange and peculiar motions, and then said he could go directly to the cows. So he started off, and went into the woods about one hundred rods distant and found the lost cows. But on finding out the secret of the mystery, Harrison had found the cows, and drove them to the above named place, and milked them. So that this stratagem turned out rather more to his profit that it did to my edification. —The old man finding that all his efforts to make me a money digger, had proved abortive, at length ceased his importunities. One circumstance, however, I will mention before leaving him. Some time before young Joseph found, or pretended to find, the gold plates, the old man told me that in Canada, there had been a book found, in a hollow tree, that gave an account of the first settlement of this country before it was discovered by Columbus.

In the month of August, 1827, I was hired by Joseph Smith, Jr. to go to Pennsylvania, to move his wife's household furniture up to Manchester, where his wife then was. When we arrived at Mr. Hale's, in Harmony, Pa. from which place he had taken his wife, a scene presented itself, truly affecting. His father-in-law (Mr. Hale) addressed Joseph, in a flood of tears: "You have stolen my daughter and married her. I had much rather have followed her to her grave. You spend your time in digging for money—pretend to see in a stone, and thus try to deceive people." Joseph wept, and acknowledged he could not see in a stone now, nor never could; and that his former pretensions in that respect, were all false. He then promised to give up his old habits of digging for money and looking into stones. Mr. Hale told Joseph, if he would move to Pennsylvania and work for a living, he would assist him in getting into business. Joseph acceded to this proposition. I then returned with Joseph and his wife to Manchester. One circumstance occurred on the road, worthy of notice, and I believe this is the only instance where Jo ever exhibited true yankee wit. On our journey to Pennsylvania, we could not make the exact change at the toll gate near Ithaca. Joseph told the gate tender, that he would "hand" him the toll on his return, as he was coming back in a few days. On our return, Joseph tendered to him 25 cents, the toll being 12 1/2. He did not recognize Smith, so he accordingly gave him back the 12 1/2 cents. After we had passed the gate, I asked him if he did not agree to pay double gatage on our return? No, said he, I agreed to "hand" it to him, and I did, but he handed it back again.

Joseph told me on his return, that he intended to keep the promise which he had made to his father-in-law; but, said he, it will be hard for me, for they will all oppose, as they want me to look in the stone for them to dig money: and in fact it was as he predicted. They urged him, day after day, to resume his old practice of looking in the stone. —He seemed much perplexed as to the course he should pursue. In this dilemma, he made me his confident and told me what daily transpired in the family of Smiths. One day he came, and greeted me with a joyful countenance. —Upon asking the cause of his unusual happiness, he replied in the following language: "As I was passing, yesterday, across the woods, after a heavy shower of rain, I found, in a hollow, some beautiful white sand, that had been washed up by the water. I took off my frock, and tied up several quarts of it, and then went home. On my entering the house, I found the family at the table eating dinner. They were all anxious to know the contents of my frock. At that moment, I happened to think of what I had heard about a history found in Canada, called the golden Bible; so I very gravely told them it was the golden Bible. To my surprise, they were credulous enough to believe what I said. Accordingly I told them that I had received a commandment to let no one see it, for, says I, no man can see it with the naked eye and live. However, I offered to take out the book and show it to them, but they refuse to see it, and left the room." Now, said Jo, "I have got the damned fools fixed, and will carry out the fun." Notwithstanding, he told me he had no such book, and believed there never was any such book, yet, he told me that he actually went to Willard Chase, to get him to make a chest, in which he might deposit his golden Bible. But, as Chase would not do it, he made a box himself, of clap-boards, and put it into a pillow case, and allowed people only to lift it, and feel of it through the case.

In the fall of 1827, Joseph wanted to go to Pennsylvania. His brother-in-law had come to assist him in moving, but he himself was out of money. He wished to borrow the money of me, and he presented Mr. Hale as security. I told him in case he could obtain assistance from no other source, I would let him have some money. Joseph then went to Palmyra; and, said he, I there met that dam fool, Martin Harris, and told him that I had a command to ask the first *honest man* I met with, for fifty dollars in money, and he would let me have it. I saw at once, said Jo, that it took his notion, for he promptly gave me the fifty.

Joseph thought this sum was sufficient to bear his expenses to Pennsylvania. So he immediately started off, and since that time I have not been much in his society. While the Smiths were living at Waterloo, William visited my neighborhood, and upon my inquiry how they came on, he replied, "we do better there than here; we were too well known here to do much.

PETER INGERSOLL.

State of New York, Wayne County, ss:

I certify, that on this 9th day of December, 1833, personally appeared before me the above named Peter Ingersoll, to me known, and made oath, according to law, to the truth of the above statement.

TH. P. BALDWIN,
Judge of Wayne County Court.

Palmyra, December 13th, 1833.

I certify that I have been personally acquainted with Peter Ingersoll for a number of years, and believe him to be a man of strict integrity, truth and veracity.

DURFEY CHASE.

9. Roswell Nichols

Manchester, Ontario County, Dec. 1st, 1833.

I, Roswell Nichols, first became acquainted with the family of Joseph Smith, Sen. nearly five years ago, and I lived a neighbor to the said family about two years. My acquaintance with the family has enabled me to know something of its character for good citizenship, probity and veracity—For breach of contracts, for the non-payment of debts and borrowed money, and for duplicity with their neighbors, the family was notorious. Once, since the Gold Bible speculation commenced, the old man was sued; and while the sheriff was at his house, he lied to him and was detected in the falsehood. Before he left the house, he confessed that it was sometimes necessary for him to tell an honest lie, in order to live. At another time, he told me that he had received an express command for me to repent and believe as he did, or I must be damned. I refused to comply, and at the same time told him of the various impositions of his family. He then stated their digging was not for money but it was for the obtaining of a Gold Bible. Thus contradicting what he had told me before: for he had often said, that the hills in our neighborhood were nearly all erected by human hands—that they were all full of gold and silver. And one time, when we were talking on the subject, he pointed to a small hill on my farm, and said, "in that hill there is a stone which is full of gold and silver. I know it to be so, for I have been to the hole, and God said unto me, *go not in now, but at a future day you shall go in and find the book open, and then you shall have the treasures.*" He said that gold and silver was once as plenty as the stones in the field are now—that the ancients, half of them melted the ore and made the gold and silver, while the other half buried it deeper in the earth, which accounted for these hills. Upon my enquiring who furnished the food for the whole, he flew into a passion, and called me a sinner, and said he, "you must be eternally damned."

I mention these facts, not because of their intrinsic importance, but simply to show the weak mindedness and low character of the man.

ROSWELL NICHOLS.

10. Barton Stafford

Manchester, Ontario Co., N.Y. Nov. 3d, 1833.

Being called upon to give a statement of the character of the family of Joseph Smith, Sen. as far as I know, I can state that I became acquainted with them in 1820, and knew them until 1831, when they left this neighborhood. —Joseph Smith, Sen. was a noted drunkard and most of the family followed his example, and Joseph, Jr. especially, who was very much addicted to intemperance. In short, not one of the family had the least claims to respectability. Even since he professed to be inspired of the Lord to translate the Book of Mormon, he one day while at work in my father's field, got quite drunk on a composition of cider, molasses and water. Finding his legs to refuse their office he leaned upon the fence and hung for sometime; at length recovering again, he fell to scuffling with one of the workmen, who tore his shirt nearly off from him. His wife who was at our house on a visit, appeared very much grieved at his conduct, and to protect his back from the rays of the sun, and conceal his nakedness, threw her shawl over his shoulders and in that plight escorted the Prophet home. As an evidence of his piety and devotion, when intoxicated, he frequently made his religion the topic of conversation!!

BARTON STAFFORD.

State of New York, Wayne County, ss:
I certify that on the 9th day of December 1833, personally appeared before me, the above named Barton Stafford, to me known, and solemnly affirmed according to law, to the truth of the above statement and subscribed the same.

THOS. P. BALDWIN,
a Judge of Wayne County Court.

11. David Stafford

Manchester, December 5th, 1833.

I have been acquainted with the family of Joseph Smith Sen. for several years, and I know him to be a drunkard and a liar, and to be much in the habit of gambling. He and his boys were truly a lazy set of fellows, and more particularly Joseph, who, very aptly followed his father's example, and in some respects was worse. When intoxicated he was very quarrelsome. Previous to his going to Pennsylvania to get married, we worked together making a coal-pit. While at work at one time, a dispute arose between us, (he having drinked a little too freely) and some hard words passed between us, and as usual with him at such times, was for fighting. He got the advantage of me in the scuffle, and a gentleman by the name of Ford interfered, when Joseph turned to fighting him. We both entered a complaint against him and he was fined for the breach of the Peace. It is well known, that the general employment of the Smith family was money digging and fortune-telling. They kept around them constantly, a gang of worthless fellows who dug for money nights, and were idle in the day time. It was a mystery to their neighbors how they got their living. I will mention some circumstances and the public may judge for themselves. At different times I have seen them come from the woods early in the morning, bringing meat which looked like mutton. I went into the woods one morning very early, shooting patridges and found Joseph Smith Sen. in company with two other men, with hoes, shovels and meat that looked like mutton. On seeing me they run like wild men to get out of sight. — Seeing the old man a few day afterwards, I asked him why he run so the other day in the woods, ah, said he, you know that circumstances alter cases; it will not do to be seen at all time.

I can also state, that Oliver Cowdrey proved himself to be a worthless person and not to be trusted or believed when he taught school in this neighborhood. After his going into the ministry, while officiating in performing the ordinance of baptism in a brook, William Smith, (brother of Joseph Smith) seeing a young man writing down what was said on a piece of board, was quite offended and attempted to take it from him, kicked at him and clinched for a scuffle. — Such was the conduct of these pretended Disciples of the Lord.

DAVID STAFFORD.

On the 12th day of December, 1833, the said David Stafford appeared before me, and made oath that the foregoing statement, by him subscribed, is true.

FRED'K. SMITH,
Justice of the Peace of Wayne Co. N.Y.

12. Joshua Stafford

Manchester, Ontario County, Nov. 15th, 1833.
I, Joshua Stafford, became acquainted with the family of Joseph Smith, Sen. about the year 1819 or 20. They then were laboring people, in low circumstances. A short time after this, they commenced digging for hidden treasures, and soon after they became indolent, and told marvellous stories about ghosts, hob-goblins, caverns, and various other mysterious matters. Joseph once showed me a piece of wood which he said he took from a

box of money, and the reason he gave for not obtaining the box, was, that it *moved*. At another time, he, (Joseph, Jr.) at a husking, called on me to become security for a horse, and said he would reward me handsomely, for he had found a box of watches, and they were as large as his fist, and he put one of them to his ear, and he could hear it "tick forty rods." Since he could not dispose of them profitably at Canandaigua or Palmyra, he wished to go east with them. He said if he did not return with the horse, I might take his life. I replied, that he knew I would not do that. Well, said he, I did not suppose you would, yet I would be willing that you should. He was nearly intoxicated at the time of the above conversation.

JOSHUA STAFFORD.

13. William Stafford

Manchester, Ontario Co. N.Y. Dec. 8th, 1833.

I, William Stafford, having been called upon to give a true statement of my knowledge, concerning the character and conduct of the family of Smiths, known to the world as the founders of the Mormon sect, do say, that I first became acquainted with Joseph, Sen., and his family in the year 1820. They lived, at that time, in Palmyra, about one mile and a half from my residence. A great part of their time was devoted to digging for money: especially in the night time, when they said the money could be most easily obtained. I have heard them tell marvellous tales, respecting the discoveries they had made in their peculiar occupation of money digging. They would say, for instance, that in such a place, in such a hill, on a certain man's farm, there were deposited keys, barrels and hogsheads of coined silver and gold — bars of gold, golden images, brass kettles filled with gold and silver — gold candlesticks, swords, &c. &c. They would say, also, that nearly all the hills in this part of New York, were thrown up by human hands, and in them were large caves, which Joseph, Jr., could see, by placing a stone of singular appearance in his hat, in such a manner as to exclude all light; at which time they pretended he could see all things within and

under the earth, —that he could see within the above mentioned
caves, large gold bars and silver plates—that he could also discover the spirits in whose charge these treasures were, clothed
in ancient dress. At certain times, these treasures could be obtained very easily; at others, the obtaining of them was difficult.
The facility of approaching them, depended in a great measure
on the state of the moon. New moon and good Friday, I believe,
were regarded as the most favorable times for obtaining these
treasures. These tales I regarded as visionary. However, being
prompted by curiosity, I at length accepted of their invitations,
to join them in their nocturnal excursions. I will now relate a few
incidents attending these excursions.

Joseph Smith, Sen., came to me one night, and told
me, that Joseph Jr. had been looking in his glass, and had seen,
not many rods from his house, two or three kegs of gold and
silver, some feet under the surface of the earth; and that none
others but the elder Joseph and myself could get them. I accordingly consented to go, and early in the evening repaired to the
place of deposit. Joseph, Sen. first made a circle, twelve or fourteen feet in diameter. This circle, said he, contains the treasure.
He then stuck in the ground a row of witch hazel sticks, around
the said circle, for the purpose of keeping off the evil spirits.
Within this circle he made another, of about eight or ten feet in
diameter. He walked around three times on the periphery of this
last circle, muttering to himself something which I could not understand. He next stuck a steel rod in the centre of the circles,
and then enjoined profound silence upon us, lest we should arouse
the evil spirit who had the charge of these treasures. After we
had dug a trench about five feet in depth around the rod, the old
man by signs and motions, asked leave of absence, and went to
the house to inquire of young Joseph the cause of our disappointment. He soon returned and said, that Joseph had remained
all this time in the house, looking in his stone and watching the
motions of the evil spirit—that he saw the spirit come up to the
ring and as soon as it beheld the cone which we had formed
around the rod, it caused the money to sink. We then went into
the house, and the old man observed, that we had made a mis-

take in the commencemnt of the operation; if it had not been for that, said he, we should have got the money.

At another time, they devised a scheme, by which they might satiate their hunger, with the mutton of one of my sheep. They had seen in my flock of sheep, a large, fat, black weather. Old Joseph and one of the boys came to me one day, and said that Joseph Jr. had discovered some very remarkable and valuable treasures, which could be procured only in one way. That way, was as follows: — That a black sheep should be taken on to the ground where the treasures were concealed — that after cutting its throat, it should be led around a circle while bleeding. This being done, the wrath of the evil spirit would be appeased: the treasures could then be obtained, and my share of them was to be four fold. To gratify my curiosity, I let them have a large fat sheep. They afterwards informed me, that the sheep was killed pursuant to commandment; but as there was some mistake in the process, it did not have the desired effect. This, I believe, is the only time they ever made money-digging a profitable business. They, however, had around them constantly a worthless gang, whose employment it was to dig money nights, and who, day times, had more to do with mutton than money.

When they found that the people of this vicinity would no longer put any faith in their schemes for digging money, they then pretended to find a gold bible, of which, they said, the book of Mormon was only an introduction. This latter book was at length fitted for the press. No means were taken by any individual to suppress its publication: No one apprehended any danger from a book, originating with individuals who had neither influence, honesty or honor. The two Josephs and Hiram, promised to show me the plates, after the book of Mormon was translated. But, afterwards, they pretended to have received an express commandment, forbidding them to show the plates. Respecting the manner of receiving and translating the book of Mormon, their statements were always discordant. The elder Joseph would say that he had seen the plates, and that he knew them to be gold; at other times he would say that they looked like gold; and other times he would say he had not seen the plates at all. I have thus briefly stated a few of the facts, in relation to the conduct and character of this family of Smiths; probably sufficient has been stated without my going into detail.

WILLIAM STAFFORD.

State of New York, Wayne County, ss:
         I certify, that on this 9th day of December, 1833, personally appeared before me, William Stafford, to me known, and made oath to the truth of the above statement, and signed the same.

TH. P. BALDWIN
Judge of Wane County Court

Palmyra, December 4th, 1833.
         I am acquainted with William Stafford and Peter Ingersoll, and believe them to be men of truth and veracity.

J. S. COLT.

Palmyra, December 4th, 1833
         We the undersigned, are personally acquainted with William Stafford, Willard Chase and Peter Ingersoll, and believe them to be men of truth and veracity.

GEORGE BECKWITH.
NATH'L. H. BECKWITH.
THOMAS ROGERS, 2D.
MARTIN W. WILCOX.

14. G. W. Stodard

Palmyra, Nov. 28th, 1833
         Having been called upon to state a few facts which are material to the characters of some of the leaders of the Mormon sect, I will do so in a concise and plain manner. I have been acquainted with Martin Harris, about thirty years. As a farmer,

he was industrious and enterprising, so much so, that he had, (previous to his going into the Gold Bible speculation) accumulated, in real estate, some eight or ten thousand dollars. Although he possessed wealth, his moral and religious character was such, as not to entitle him to respect among his neighbors. He was fretful, peevish and quarrelsome, not only in the neighborhood, but in his family. He was known to frequently abuse his wife, by whipping her, kicking her out of bed and turning her out of doors &c. Yet he was a public professor of some religion. He was first an orthadox Quaker, then a Universalist, next a Restorationer, then a Baptist, next a Presbyterian, and then a Mormon. By his willingness to become all things unto all men, he has attained a high standing among his Mormon brethren. The Smith family never made any pretentions to respectability.

G. W. STODARD.

I hereby concur in the above statement.

RICHARD H. FORD.

II. GROUP AFFIDAVITS (ARRANGED CHRONOLOGICALLY):

1. Manchester, New York, affidavit

Manchester Nov. 3d, 1833.

We, the undersigned, being personally acquainted with the family of Joseph Smith, sen. with whom the celebrated Gold Bible, so called, originated, state: that they were not only a lazy, indolent set of men, but also intemperate; and their word was not to be depended upon; and that we are truly glad to dispense with their society.

Pardon Butts,	James Gee,	Joseph Fish,
Warden A. Reed,	Abel Chase,	Horace N. Barnes,
Hiram Smith,	A. H. Wentworth,	Silvester Worden.
Alfred Stafford,	Moses C. Smith,	

2. Palmyra, New York, affidavit

Palmyra, Dec. 4, 1833.

We, the undersigned, have been acquainted with the Smith family, for a number of years, while they resided near this place, and we have no hesitation in saying, that we consider them destitute of that moral character, which ought to entitle them to the confidence of any community. They were particularly famous for visionary projects, spent much of their time in digging for money which they pretended was hid in the earth; and to this day, large excavations may be seen in the earth, not far from their residence, where they used to spend their time in digging for hidden treasures. Joseph Smith, Senior, and his son Joseph, were in particular, considered entirely destitute of *moral character, and addicted to vicious habits.*

Martin Harris was a man who had acquired a handsome property, and in matters of business his word was considered good; but on moral and religious subjects, he was perfectly visionary—sometimes advocating one sentiment, and sometimes another. And in reference to all with whom we were acquainted, that have embraced Mormonism from this neighborhood, we are compeled to say, were very visionary, and most of them destitute of moral character, and without influence in this community; and this may account why they were permitted to go on with their impositions undisturbed. It was not supposed that any of them were possessed of sufficient character or influence to make any one believe their book or their sentiments, and we know not of a single individual in this vicinity that puts the least confidence in their pretended revelations.

Geo. N. Williams,	H. Linnell,	Thos. Rogers, 2d.
Clark Robinson,	Jas. Jenner,	Wm. Parke,
Lemael Durfee,	S. Ackley,	Josiah Francis,
E. S. Townsend,	Josiah Rice,	Ames Hollister,
Henry P. Alger,	Jesse Townsend,	G. A. Hathaway,
C. E. Thayer,	Rich'd. D. Clark,	David G. Ely,
G. W. Anderson,	Th. P. Baldwin,	H. K. Jerome,
H. P. Thayer,	John Sothington,	G. Beckwith

L. Williams,	Durfey Chase,	Lewis Foster,
Geo. W. Crosby,	Wells Anderson,	Hiram Payne,
Levi Thayer,	N. H. Beckwith,	P. Grandin,
R. S. Williams,	Philo Durfee	L. Hurd,
P. Sexton,	Giles. S. Ely,	Joel Thayer,
M. Butterfield,	R. W. Smith,	E. D. Robinson,
S. P. Seymour,	Pelatiah West,	Asahel Millard,
D. S. Jackways,	Henry Jessup,	A. Ensworth,
John Hurlbut,	Linus North,	Israel F. Chilson,

III. MISCELLANEOUS INDIVIDUAL AFFIDAVITS (ARRANGED ALPHABETI-
CALLY ACCORDING TO SURNAME OF TESTATOR):

1. Alva Hale

ALVA HALE, son of Isaac Hale, states, that Joseph Smith Jr. told him that his (Smith's) gift in seeing with a stone and hat, was a gift from God," but also states "that Smith told him at another time that this *"peeping"* was all d––-d nonsense. He (Smith) was deceived himself but did not intend to deceive others; –that he intended to quit the business, (of peeping) and labor for his livelihood." That afterwards, Smith told him, he should see the Plates from which he translated the book of Mormon," and accordingly at the time specified by Smith, he (Hale) "called to see the plates, but Smith did not show them, but appeared angry." He further states, that he knows Joseph Smith Jr. to be an impostor, and a liar, and knows Martin Harris to be a liar likewise.

2. Levi Lewis

LEVI LEWIS states, that he has "been acquainted with Joseph Smith Jr. and Martin Harris, and that he has heard them both say, adultery was no crime. Harris said he did not blame Smith for his (Smith's) attempt to seduce Eliza Winters &c.;"– Mr. Lewis says that he "knows Smith to be a liar; –that he saw him (Smith) intoxicated at three different times while he was composing the Book of Mormon, and also that he has heard Smith when driving oxen, use language of the greatest profanity. Mr. Lewis also testifies that he heard Smith say he (Smith) was as good as Jesus Christ; —that it was as bad to injure him as it was to injure Jesus Christ." "With regard to the plates, Smith said God had deceived him—which was the reason he (Smith) did not show them."

3. Nathaniel Lewis

March 21st, 1834.

Elder Lewis also certifies and affirms in relation to Smith as follows:

"I have been acquainted with Joseph Smith Jr. for some time: being a relation of his wife, and residing near him, I have had frequent opportunities of conversation with him, and of knowing his opinions and pursuits. From my standing in the Methodist Episcopal Church, I suppose he was careful how he conducted or expressed himself before me. At one time, however, he came to my house, and asked my advice, whether he should proceed to translate the Book of Plates (referred to by Mr. Hale) or not. He said that God had commanded him to translate it, but he was afraid of the people: he remarked, that he was to exhibit the plates to the world, at a certain time, which was then about eighteen months distant. I told him I was not qualified to give advice in such cases. Smith frequently said to me that I should see the plates at the time appointed.

After the time stipulated, had passed away, Smith being at my house was asked why he did not fulfil his promise, show the Golden Plates and prove himself an honest man? He replied that he, himself was deceived, but that I should see them if I were where they were. I reminded him then, that I stated at the time he made the promise, I was fearful "the enchantment would be so powerful" as to remove the plates, when the time came in which they were to be revealed.

"These circumstances and many others of a similar tenor, embolden me to say that Joseph Smith Jr. is not a man of truth and veracity; and that his general character in this part of the country, is that of an impostor, hypocrite and liar.

NATHANIEL C. LEWIS."

Affirmed and subscribed, before me, March 20th, 1834.

CHARLES DIMON, *J. Peace*.

4. Sophia Lewis

SOPHIA LEWIS, certifies that she "heard a conversation between Joseph Smith Jr., and the Rev. James B. Roach, in which Smith called Mr. R. a d—-d fool. Smith also said in the same conversation that he (Smith) was as good as Jesus Christ;" and that she "has frequently heard Smith use profane language. She states that she heard Smith say "the Book of Plates could not be opened under penalty of death by any other person but his (Smith's) first-born, which was to be a male." She says she "was present at the birth of this child, and that it was still-born and very much deformed."

5. Joshua M'Kune

Joshua M'Kune states, that he "was acquainted with Joseph Smith Jr. and Martin Harris, during their residence in Harmony, Pa., and knew them to be artful seducers;"—That they informed him that "Smith had found a sword, breast-plate, and a pair of spectacles, at the time he found the gold plates"—that these were to be shown to all the world as evidence of the truth of what was contained in those plates," and that "he (M'Kune) and others should see them at a specified time." He also states that "the time for the exhibition of the Plates, &c. has gone by, and he has not seen them." "Joseph Smith, Jr. told him that (Smith's) first-born child was to translate the characters, and hieroglyphics, upon the Plates into our language at the age of three years; but this child was not permitted to live to verify the prediction." He also states, that "he has been intimately acquainted with Isaac Hale twenty-four years, and has always found him to be a man of truth, and good morals."

6. Hezekiah M'Kune

HEZEKIAH M'KUNE states, that "in conversation with Joseph Smith Jr., he (Smith) said he was nearly equal to Jesus Christ; that he was a prophet sent by God to bring in the Jews, and that he was the greatest prophet that had ever arisen."

B. THE ARTHUR B. DEMING NEW YORK AFFIDAVITS, FROM: *NAKED TRUTHS ABOUT MORMONISM* (OAKLAND, CALIFORNIA), VOLUMES 1 (JANUARY 1888) AND 2 (APRIL 1888) (ARRANGED ALPHABETICALLY ACCORDING TO SURNAME OF TESTATOR)

1. Mrs. S. F. Anderick

I was born in New York State near the Massachusetts line, May 7, 1809. In 1812 my parents moved to a farm two miles from the village, and in the township of Palmyra, New York. In 1823 mother died, and I went to her sister's, Mrs. Earl Wilcox, where I lived much of the time until December, 1828, when I went to live with father who had again married and settled on a farm on the Holland Patent, twenty miles west of Rochester, New York. Uncle Earl's farm was four miles south of Palmyra village, and his house was nearly opposite old Jo Smith's, father of the Mormon prophet. Old Jo was dissipated. He and his son Hyrum worked some at coopering. Hyrum was the only son sufficiently educated to teach school. I attended when he taught in the log schoolhouse east of uncle's. He also taught in the Stafford District. He and Sophronia were the most respected of the family, who were not much thought of in the community. They cleared the timber from only a small part of their farm, and never paid for the land. They tried to live without work. I have often heard the neighbors say they did not know how the Smiths lived, they earned so little money. The farmers who lived near the Smiths had many sheep and much poultry stolen. They often sent officers to search the premises of the Smiths for stolen property, who usually found the house locked. It was said the creek near the house of the Smiths was lined with the feet and heads of sheep. Uncle's children were all sons, and they played with Smith's younger children, I associated much with Sophronia Smith, the oldest daughter, as she was the only girl near my age who lived in our vicinity. I often accompanied her, Hyrum, and young Jo Smith, who became the Mormon prophet, to apple parings and parties. Jo was pompous, pretentious and active at parties. He claimed, when a young man, he could tell where lost or hidden things and treasures were buried or located with a forked witch hazel. He deceived many farmers, and induced them to dig nights for chests of gold, when the pick struck the chest, someone usually spoke, and Jo would say the enchantment was broken, and the chest would leave.

Williard Chase, a Methodist who lived about two miles from uncle's, while digging a well, found a gray smooth stone about the size and shape of an egg. Sallie, Williard's sister, also a Methodist, told me several times that young Jo Smith, who became the Mormon prophet, often came to inquire of her where to dig for treasures. She told me she would place the stone in a hat and hold it to her face, and claimed things would be brought to her view. Sallie let me have it several times, but I never could see anything in or through it. I heard that Jo obtained it and called it a peep-stone, which he used in the place of the witch hazel. Uncle refused to let Jo dig on his farm. I have seen many holes where he dug on other farms.

When Jo joined the Presbyterian Church, in Palmyra village, it caused much talk and surprise, as he claimed to receive revelations from the Lord. He also claimed he found some gold plates with characters on them, in a hill between uncle's and father's, which I often crossed. Several times I saw what he claimed were the plates, which were covered with a cloth. They appeared to be six or eight inches square. He frequently carried them with him. I heard they kept them under the brick hearth.

He was from home much summers. Sometimes he

said he had been to Broome County, New York, and Pennsylvania. Several times while I was visiting Sophronia Smith at old Jo's house, she told me that a stranger who I saw there several times in warm weather and several months apart, was Mr. Rigdon. At other times the Smith children told me that Mr. Rigdon was at their house when I did not see him. I did not read much in the "Book of Mormon" because I had no confidence in Jo. Palmyra people claimed that Jo did not know enough to be the author of the "Book of Mormon," and believed that Rigdon was its author. I was acquainted with most of the people about us, and with Martin Harris.

On my way to California I stopped in Salt Lake City from July, 1852, until March, 1853. I received much attention from Mormon ladies because I was acquainted, and had danced with their prophet.

[Signed.] Mrs. S. F. ANDERICK.
[Seal]

Witnessed by:
MRS. I. A. ROGERS (Daughter)
OSCAR G. ROGERS (Grandson).

Subscribed and sworn before F. S. Baker, Notary Public for Monterey County, California, June 24, 1887.

2. Isaac Butts

I was born in Palmyra, N.Y., near where old Jo Smith settled, January 4, 1807. I attended school with Prophet Jo. His father taught me to mow. I worked with old and young Jo at farming. I have frequently seen old Jo drunk. Young Jo had a forked witch-hazel rod with which he claimed he could locate buried money or hidden things. Later he had a peep-stone which he put into his hat and looked into it. I have seen both. Joshua Stafford, a good citizen, told me that young Jo Smith and himself dug for money in his orchard and elsewhere nights. All the money digging was done nights. I saw the holes in the orchard which were four or five feet square and three or four feet deep. Jo and others dug much about Palmyra and Manchester. I have seen many of the holes. The first thing he claimed to find was gold plates of the "Book of Mormon," which he kept in a pillow-case and would let people lift, but not see. I came to Ohio in 1818, and became acquainted with Sydney Rigdon in 1820. He preached my brother's funeral sermon in Auburn, O., in May, 1822. I returned to Palmyra twice and resided there about two years each time. Many persons whom I knew in New York joined the Mormons and came to Kirtland. They told me they saw Sidney Rigdon much with Jo Smith before they became Mormons, but did not know who he was until they came to Kirtland.

> [Signed.] ISAAC BUTTS.
> *South Newbury, Geauga Co, O.*

3. W. R. Hine

I was born February 11, 1803, at Colesville, Windsor Township, Broome County, N.Y. Jo Smith, who became the Mormon prophet, and his father came from Palmyra, or Manchester, N.Y., and dug for salt two summers, near and in sight of my house. The old settlers used to buy salt from an Indian squaw, who often promised to tell the whites where the salt spring was, but she never did. Jo Smith claimed to be a seer. He had a very clear stone about the size and shape of a duck's egg, and claimed that he could see lost or hidden things through it. He said he saw Captain Kidd sailing on the Susquehanna River during a freshet, and that he buried two pots of gold and silver. He claimed he saw writing cut on the rocks in an unknown language telling where Kidd buried it, and he translated it through his peep-stone. I have had it many times and could see in it whatever I imagined. Jo claimed it was found in digging a well in Palmyra, N.Y. He said he borrowed it. He claimed to receive revelations from the Lord through prayer, and would pray with his men, mornings and at other times. His father told me he was fifteen years old. I called him half-witted. He was miserably clad, coarse and awkward. He had men who did the digging and they and others would take interests. Some would lose faith and others would take their places. They dug one well thirty feet deep and another seventy-five at the foot and south side of the Aquaga Mountain, but found no salt.

My nephew now owns the land he dug on. Asa Stowel furnished the means for Jo to dig for silver ore, on Monument Hill. He dug over one year without success. Jo dug next for Kidd's money, on the west bank of the Susquehanna, half a mile from the river, and three miles from his salt wells. He dug for a cannon the Indians had buried, until driven away by the owner of the land. He dug for many things and many parties, I never knew him to find anything of value. He and his workmen lived in a shanty while digging for salt. When it rained hard, my wife has often made beds for them on the floor in our house. Jo became known all over New York and Pennsylvania. Sometimes his brothers were with him. Isaac Hale, a good Methodist, lived seven miles below me on the river. I often stopped with him when rafting. I have attended many prayer-meetings at his house, evenings. Emma was fine looking, smart, a good singer, and she often got the power. Jo stole his wife, Sunday, while Hale was at church. My wife and I saw him on an old horse with Emma on behind as they passed our house on their way to Bainbridge, N.Y., where they were married.

Jo and his father were all the time telling of hidden things, lead, silver and gold mines which he could see. I called him Peeker. About the spring of 1828, Jo came in front of my house where several men were pitching quoits. I said, "Peeker, what have you found?" He said he had found some metal plates which would be of great use to the world. He had them in a box in a handkerchief which he carried in one hand. I said, "Let me see them." Jo Smith said they must first be sent to Philadelphia to be translated. He said the only man in the world who could translate them lived there. After they were translated the world could see them. Calvin Smith, whose farm joined mine, said with an oath, he would see them. Jo said if he laid his hands on him he would prosecute him. I told Calvin he better not. Since I have seen the conduct of the Mormons, I have many times regretted that I interfered. Citizens wrote to parties in Philadelphia, where Jo said he had sent the plates and word was returned they had not received them. Jo said they could not be translated in Philadelphia and they had been sent to New York City. Justice N. K. Nobles wrote to New York and could learn nothing about them. Soon I learned that Jo claimed to be translating the plates in Badger's Tavern, in Colesville, three miles from my house. I went there and saw Jo Smith sit by a table and put a handkerchief to his forehead and peek into his hat and call out a word to Cowdery, who sat at the same table and wrote it down. Several persons sat near the same table and there was no curtain between them. Martin Harris introduced himself to me, and said they were going to bring the world from darkness into light. Martin's wife cooked for them, and one day while they were at dinner she put one hundred and sixteen pages, the first part they had translated, in her dress bosom and went out. They soon missed the one hundred and sixteen pages and followed her into the road and demanded them of her. She refused, and said if it was the Lord's work you can translate them again, and I will follow you to the ends of the earth.

Dr. Seymour came along and she gave them to him to read, and told him not to let them go. Dr. Seymour lived one and a half miles from me. He read most of it to me when my daughter Irene was born; he read them to his patients about the country. It was a description of the mounds about the country and similar to the "Book of Mormon." I doubt if the one hundred and sixteen pages were included in the "Book of Mormon." After I came to Kirtland, in conversation with Martin Harris, he has many times admitted to me that this statement about his wife and the one hundred and sixteen pages, as above stated, is true. I heard a man say who was a neighbor to the Mormon Smith family, in Palmyra, N.Y., that they were thieves, indolent, the lowest and meanest family he ever saw or heard of. Hyrum was the best of the family. Many letters were received from Palmyra, stating the bad character of the Smith's. Calvin Smith and I, while burning brush, found a hole which, when cleaned out, was fifteen feet deep; it was covered with poles which had been split with tomahawks; a tree near by was marked each side for seventy feet. Gun barrels and various Indian implements were found later near by. The hole was within twenty rods of Jo's salt digging. Newel Knight, who lived a few miles from me was brought before Justice N. K. Nobles as a witness for reporting Prophet Jo Smith had cast three devils out of him. Knight testified the first was as large as a wood chuck, the second was as large as a squirrel, the third about the size of a rat. Noble inquired what became of them. Knight said that they went out at the chimney. Jo was discharged. Noble told me later that it made his heart ache to hear the puppy swear. This occurred during the pretended translation of the plates. I met Prophet Jo's father on the dock at Fairport, O., in July, 1831. He inquired if I came on in the Mormon faith, I replied that I did: a crowd soon gathered about us. One of them asked what my faith was. I said the Mormons were the damd'st set of liars and scoundrels I ever knew. My reply caused a shout from many on the dock. We all took a drink.

I rented Claudius Stannard's farm and stone quarry, two miles south of the temple in Kirtland. (Before I rented the quarry, a combination had been formed not to let the Mormons have any stone). I quarried and sold the Mormons the stone used in the construction of the temple, except a few of the large ones which came from Russell's quarry. Prophet Jo and his father frequently talked over with me their experience along the Susquehanna. Jo could scarcely read or write when he lived in New York. He had a private teacher in Kirtland and obtained a fair education. While the temple was building the workmen lived in temporary buildings. Prayer meetings were held mornings by the workmen for the success of the work before beginning their labors. One day while I was at the Flats, a meeting was held in which the Spiritual Wife Doctrine was discussed. Rigdon said if he had got to go into it he might as well begin. He put Emma, Jo Smith's wife, on the bed and got on himself. Jo became angry. It was in everybody's mouth for miles about Kirtland. When I first saw Emma on the streets in Kirtland, she threw her arms around me and I think kissed me, and inquired all about her father's family. I brought her letters and took some later to Mr. Hale from her. Jo told Emma he had a revelation about the plates, but that he could not obtain them until he had married her. I became acquainted with D. P. Hurlbut before he left the Mormons. He courted Dr. Williams' beautiful daughter, and told her he had a revelation to marry her; she told him when she received a revelation they would be married. Everybody about Kirtland believed he had left the Mormons because she refused him. Other Mormons and Black Pete claimed to receive revelations to marry her. I was often in Hurlbut's company, and once while fishing with him on Lake Erie, after he had left the Mormons, he told me he was going to ferret out Mormonism and break it up; I replied you had better break up a nest of yellow jackets. I told him I knew the Mormons in New York State would as soon swear to a lie as to the truth. Later I told Hurlbut to write to Isaac Hale, Jo's father-in-law, and he did.

Hale's reply is published in Howe's "Book on Mormonism." I heard Hurlbut lecture in the Presbyterian Church in Kirtland. He said he *would*, and he *did prove* that the "Book of Mormon" was founded on a fiction called "Manuscript Found," written by Solomon Spaulding, at Conneaut, Ohio, in the early part of the century. He said Spaulding was consumptive and could not work, and wrote stories to procure a living. He said he had seen Mrs. Spaulding, and she said a good share of the "Book of Mormon" was the same as "Manuscript Found," which was written by her husband, Solomon Spaulding. Spaulding's brother asked him, as he was an educated man, why he wrote in old style. He said his title was "Manuscript Found" and therefore he wrote it in old style. Hurlbut said Spaulding tried to obtain money to pay for printing it. While traveling he slept in the woods nights, took cold and finally died. Sydney Rigdon stole the copy left with the printer in Pittsburgh. Hurlbut had a copy of Spaulding's "Manuscript Found" with him. He and others spoke three hours. Hurlbut read Hale's letter in the lecture. Martin Harris said Hale was old and blind and not capable of writing it. I stated that Hale was called the greatest hunter on the Susquehanna, and two years before had killed a black deer and a white bear, which many hunters had tried to kill, also that he was intelligent and knew the Scriptures. The night the meteors fell in 1833, the Mormons sent men on horseback for miles about Kirtland to arouse the people. They got me up at three o'clock A.M., they claimed it was the fore-runner of some wonderful event, and it was said and believed. Prophet Jo said there would be no more stars seen in the heavens. All the time I was in Kirtland many persons were becoming disgusted with Mormonism, and many left them and exposed their secrets. Squire J. C. Dowen lived half a mile from me, he was physically and mentally a capable man. His reputation as a citizen was very good. This statement was read to me and my daughter before being signed. I heard Hurlbut lecture before, and after he saw Spaulding's widow.

W. R. HINE X.

Witnessed by:
A. B. Deming
Chester, Geauga County, Ohio

4. Joseph Rogers

I was born in Wester, Oneida Co., N.Y., Feb. 10, 1805. Our family moved to Phelpstown a few miles south of Palmyra, N.Y., in 1815, where I resided until 1842. I was often in Palmyra, and was well acquainted with Jo Smith, who became the Mormon prophet. When a young man he claimed to receive revelations from the Lord where treasures were buried. He told Peter Rupert and Mr. Cunningham, a blacksmith (simple-minded old men), that there was a chest of gold buried on my brother-in-law, Henry Murphy's farm, under a beech tree. Henry's younger brother, Jack, said that must be stopped, and he obtained some filth in a sap bucket and got up in the beech tree before they arrived in the evening. They came and Mr. Rupert held the Bible open and a lighted candle as prophet Jo directed, while Peter dug for the chest of gold. Jack called Peter three times and he looked up and said, "Here am I, Lord," and received the filth in his face. Peter told me and others that the Lord chastised him and he had to stop his digging. He said he paid Jo for the information. I told him he ought not to believe Jo, for he was liar and imposter. He said Jo would put a spell on him and that he would have to stand still two weeks. He said Jo had perfect command over men. He believed he was a prophet. Jack was called Lord Murphy afterwards. There were many others similarly duped by Jo. Many of Jo's victims were from New Jersey and believed in witches and ghosts. He could not fool the New England or York State Yankees. Jo Smith and his adherents dug a cave in a hill in Manchester, N.Y., and used to go there, he said, to consult with the Lord. He had a door at the entrance fastened with a padlock. The sheriff took possession and found much property which had been stolen from farmers about there. Jo had left for Ohio. It was believed that Jo intended to remove the property.

I had the affidavits of six creditable farmers who lived in Manchester, N.Y., that Jo Smith, who became the Mormon prophet, stole their chickens and sheep. I lost them moving. Farmers said he was a terror to the neighborhood and that he would either have to go to State prison, be hung, or leave the county, or he would be killed. Jo contrived in every way to obtain money without work. The farmers claimed that not a week passed without Jo stole something. I knew at least one hundred farmers in the towns of Phelps, Manchester and Palmyra, N.Y., who would make oath that Jo Smith the Mormon prophet was a liar, intemperate and a base imposter. His father, old Jo, was called a devil. He was very intemperate, profane and vulgar in conversation. Jo, the prophet, said much about his troubles with the devil and that he, the devil, got the better of him much of the time. Jo traveled about the country considerable and was well known.

While visiting my uncle, Jacob Wiggins, in Western, Oneida Co., N.Y., I attended a Mormon meeting in a schoolhouse about three miles north of Rome, N.Y. The preacher spoke about twenty minutes and then introduced a woman who would speak in the unknown tongue. She said, "Feel of me low, feel of me lee, feel of me li." A man by the door got up and said, "By — — I can interpret it: Feel of my toe, feel of my knee, feel of my thigh. That is what she means," and left the room. He was under the influence of liquor. It caused so much laughter it stopped the meeting. My uncle always laughed when I asked him about the unknown tongue. My uncle knew the interpreter. I was informed by three or four creditable parties who were at a public house in the town of Pittsford, Ontario Co., N.Y., that a stranger stayed over night and died as was supposed. A doctor was called and another stranger soon came. He said he was a Mormon and could bring the dead to life. The hotel keeper requested him to restore the man to life. The doctor inquired if he could if the man's head was cut off. The Mormon replied he could. The doctor took an ax and said he would cut off his head. The pretended dead man rose up and said, "For God's sake don't cut off my head." I have no doubt the above is true, knowing the persons well who informed me. But few persons about Palmyra and Manchester became Mormons. Jo, the prophet, pretended to tell fortunes for pay. He could read the character of men readily and could tell who he could dupe.

[Signed] JOSEPH ROGERS.
[Seal]

Witnessed by:
HELEN ROGERS (Daughter).
Los Gatos, Cal, May 16, 1887.

Subscribed and sworn to before me this 16th day of May, A.D., 1887.

JOHN F. TOBIN,
Notary Public.

5. Lorenzo Saunders
HILLSDALE COUNTY, State of Michigan.
Lorenzo Saunders being duly sworn deposes and says:
That I reside in Reading, Hillsdale County, State of Michigan; that I was born in the town of Palmyra, Wayne County, State of

New York, on June 7, A.D. 1811, and am now seventy-six years of age. That I lived in said town of Palmyra until I was forty-three years of age. That I lived within one mile of Joseph Smith at the time said Joseph Smith claimed that he found the "tablets" on which the "Book of Mormon" was revealed. That I went to the "Hill Cumorah" on the Sunday following the date that Joseph Smith claimed he found the plates, it being three miles from my home, and I tried to find the place where the earth had been broken by being dug up, but was unable to find any place where the ground had been disturbed.

That my father died on the 10th day of October, A.D. 1825. That in March of 1827, on or about the 15th of said month I went to the house of Joseph Smith for the purpose of getting some maple sugar to eat, that when I arrived at the house of said Joseph Smith, I was met at the door by Harrison Smith, Jo's brother. That at a distance of ten or twelve rods from the house there were five men that were engaged in talking, four of whom I knew, the fifth one was better dressed than the rest of those whom I was acquainted with. I inquired of Harrison Smith who the stranger was? He informed me his name was Sidney Rigdom with whom I afterwards became acquainted and found to be Sidney Rigdon. This was in March, A.D. 1827, the second spring after the death of my father. I was frequently at the house of Joseph Smith from 1827 to 1830. That I saw Oliver Cowdery writing, I suppose the "Book of Mormon" with books and manuscript laying on the table before him; that I went to school to said Oliver Cowdery and knew him well. That in the summer of 1830, I heard Sydney Rigdon preach a sermon on Mormonism. This was after the "Book of Mormon" had been published, which took about three years from the time that Joseph Smith claimed to have had his revelation.

[Signed.] LORENZO SAUNDERS
[Seal.]

Sworn and subscribed to before me this 21st day of July, A.D. 1887.

LINUS S. PARMELEE,
Justice of the Peace of Reading, Mich.

6. Henry A. Sayer

. . . My parents desired their children to be American citizens, and imigrated in 1816 to Luzerne County, Pa., seven miles from Wilkesbarre. When a young man I spent much of the summers along the Susquehanna River. I became acquainted with Jo, Hyrum, and Bill Smith, whom I often saw hunting and digging for buried money, treasure, or lost and hidden things. Jo claimed to receive revelations from the Lord where to dig. People would say, "Jo, what did the Lord tell you last night, or what did you dream?" "Jo, what are you going to dig for next?" "Jo, I found a hollow tree or stump; go and see what you can find there." He had a peep-stone which he claimed had an attraction, and he could see hidden things through it. He was generally called the Peeker. He was said to be the laziest whelp about the country. He had men to do the digging. I have heard merchants refuse to trust Jo Smith for a plug of tobacco, but say they would give him one. I well remember when he organized his Mormon Church at Harmony, Pa. My father said at the time that Mormonism would take well with the ignorant English, and would become troublesome in this country. He claimed the Government ought to put a stop to it.

HENRY A. SAYER

Witnessed by:
A. B. DEMING.

Subscribed and sworn to before me at Willoughby this twenty-fourth day of February, 1885.

A. P. BARBER,
Justice of the Peace in and of Lake County, Ohio

7. Mrs. M. C. R. Smith

I was born in Belchertown, Mass., May 1, 1812. When I was five or six years old my parents moved to Manchester, N.Y., one mile from the Mormon Smith family, and I attended school with their children. There was considerable digging for money in our neighborhood by men, women and children. I never knew of their finding any. I saw a large hole dug on Nathaniel Smith's farm, which was sandy. I saw Joshua Stafford's peep-stone which looked like white marble and had a hole through the center. Sallie Chase, a Methodist, had one and people would go for her to find lost and hidden or stolen things. My mother was one of the first Mormon converts. Father copied the "Book of Mormon" for the printer, or part of it. I heard Martin Harris say that the first part of the "Book of Mormon" was stolen and that he thought his wife took it and it was not printed in the "Book of Mormon." Father joined the Mormons after my parents went West. Catherine Smith, sister of the prophet, showed me in their house a chest with lock where the plates were kept, but they feared they would be stolen, and then she took up four bricks in the hearth and said they had been buried there. Jo Smith's mother doctored many persons in Palmyra. My sister, with whom mother died in California, was opposed to her being a Mormon. I hope sometime it will be known whether Mormonism is true or not. My brother, Orrin Porter Rockwell, made me a visit in 1844 or '45. When ten years old he broke his leg and a young doctor in Palmyra set it so one leg was shorter than the other and it always troubled him so he could not work at farming.

[Signed] MRS. M. C. R. SMITH.

Witnessed by:
A. B. DEMING,
B. N. SHAW.
Hamden, Ohio, March 25, 1885.

8. Christopher M. Stafford

I was born in Manchester, Ontario Co., N.Y., May 26, 1808. I well remember about 1820, when old Jo Smith and family settled on one hundred acres one mile north of our house. The north line of his farm was the boundary line between Manchester, Ontario Co., and Palmyra, Wayne Co.; N.Y. The village of Palmyra was about two miles north of Jo's house. Old Jo claimed to be a cooper but worked very little at anything. He was intemperate. Hyrum worked at cooperage. Alvin was the oldest son and worked the farm and was the stay of the family. He died a few years after they came. I exchanged work with Jo but more with his brother Harrison, who was a good, industrous boy. I did not enjoy my meals at the Smith's, they were so filthy. Jo got drunk while we were haying for my uncle, Wm. Stafford; also at a husking at our house, and stayed overnight. I have often seen him drunk. Jo was the laziest one of the family, and a dull scholar, as were all the Smiths except Harrison and Catherine. I attended school with them, also Bill and Carlos.

Oliver Cowdery taught one winter. Catherine's reputation for virtue was not good. Jo claimed he could tell where money was buried, with a witch hazel consisting of a forked stick of hazel. He held it one fork in each hand and claimed the upper end was attracted by the money. I heard my stepfather, Robert Orr, say he had been digging for money one night. Some of my neighbors also said they were digging for money nights. My mother-in-law, Mrs. Rockwell, said that Prophet Jo Smith told her there was money buried in the ground and she spent considerable time digging in various places for it. I never knew of her finding any. Jo Smith told me there was a peep-stone for me and many others if we could only find them. Jo claimed to have revelations and tell fortunes. He told mine by looking in the palm of my hand and said among other things that I would not live to be very old.

When he claimed to find gold plates of the Mormon Bible no attention was paid to them or him by his neighbors. Some time after Jo had men dig on a tunnel forty or fifty feet long in a hill about two miles north of where he claimed to find the plates. I have been in it. Some people surmised it was intended for counterfeiting. Jo was away much of the time summers. He claimed to have a revelation that Manchester, N.Y., was to be destroyed and all the Mormons must leave for Kirkland, O. Orrin Rockwell and wife wanted my wife, their daughter, to go to Missouri. We came to Auburn, Geauga Co., O., Dec. 2, 1831, and have since resided here.

Orrin Porter Rockwell made us a visit on a fine horse (I doubt if he owned it). Soon after Governor Boggs was shot. Prophet Jo told Mrs. Risley, of Manchester, a cripple, he could heal her and she joined the Mormons. Jo failed to heal her and she never walked.

[Signed] C. M. STAFFORD.

Witnessed by:
A. B. DEMING.
Auburn, March 23, 1885.

9. Cornelius R. Stafford

I was born in Manchester, New York, Feb. 4, 1813. Our school district was called the Stafford District because of sixty scholars enrolled, forty were Staffords. The road on which they lived is now called Stafford Street. The Mormon Smith family lived near our house. I was well acquainted with them and attended school with the younger children. There was much digging for money on our farm and about the neighborhood. I saw Uncle John and Cousin Joshua Stafford dig a hole twenty feet long, eight broad and seven deep. They claimed that they were digging for money but were not successful in finding any. Jo Smith kept it up after our neighbors had abandoned it. A year or two after Jo claimed to find the plates of the "Book of Mormon." He had men dig a tunnel near fifty feet long in a hill about two miles north of the hill where he claimed to find the plates. I tried to look into a peep-stone in my hat in a dark room; I saw nothing, some claimed they could. I saw old Jo Smith, his wife and Mrs. Rockwell baptized by prophet Jo Smith. I have seen Jo in drunken fights; father and son were frequently drunk. I remember when a man (Hurlbut) came to our school house and took statements about the bad character of the Mormon Smith family, and saw them swear to them. Jo Smith, the prophet, told my uncle, William Stafford, he wanted a fat, black sheep. He said he wanted to cut its throat and make it walk in a circle three times around and it would prevent a pot of money from leaving. Jo's family ate the sheep; he duped many people in similar ways. He claimed to receive revelations from the Lord. The Smiths stole six hogs-heads from us; everything missing was claimed by our neighbors to be in possession of the Smiths. I would make oaths to my statement were not the Justice sick.

[Signed.] C. R. STAFFORD

Witnessed by:
R. M. STAFFORD (Son)
INA M. RICHARDS (G. daughter).
Auburn, O., March, 1885.

10. Mrs. Sylvia Walker

I was born in Manchester, Ontario County, N.Y., Aug. 27, 1818, and lived there until 1852, when I came to Ohio. The Mormon Smith family lived in sight of my parents' house. I attended school to Oliver Cowdrey with Carlos, Sam, Bill, Catherine, and Lucy Smith, who were very poor scholars. Jo, Hyrum and Sophrona, the other children, were older. I have been at their house. They were the lowest family I ever knew. They worked very little and had the reputation of stealing everything they could lay their hands on. Old Jo was very intemperate. When Jo told his neighbors about finding gold plates no one believed him nor paid any attention to it, he had humbugged them so much. Much of the time he claimed he was in Pennsylvania. I attended a Mormon meeting in old Jo Smith's loghouse.

Martin Harris spoke and Darius Pearse laughed at something he said. He reproved Pearse, who left the house, and when he was in the road began to denounce the Smith family and talked nearly one hour. The audience left the house and listened to him. He reviewed the character of them and said they stole six of his fat sheep. His talk greatly pleased his neighbors. He was one of our best citizens. The Mormons said the price of the "Book of Mormon" was established at $1.75 by revelation. It did not sell well and they claimed to receive another to sell it at $1.25. The people were amused that the Mormon Deity did not know what price to set upon the book. It was freely talked among the neighbors that Jo Smith said he had a revelation to go to Pennsylvania and get him a wife. Jo claimed to receive a revelation to dig forty feet into a hill about two miles north of where he pretended to find the gold plates of the "Book of Mormon," where he would find a cave that contained gold furniture, chairs and table. The Mormons dug into the hill horizontally over forty feet without finding any cave. The boys troubled them so they placed a door with lock at the entrance. The boys placed brush against it and destroyed it with fire. The Mormons abandoned it. I heard our neighbors say probably Jo Smith dug his fat sheep and barrels of flour out of it.

[Signed] MRS. SYLVIA WALKER.

Witnessed by:
MRS. ALBERT PHINNEY
(Daughter).
MISS LULA PHINNEY
(Granddaughter).
Chester, Ohio, March 20, 1885.

C. A TYPESCRIPT OF THE HANDWRITTEN NOTES OF THE 1881 WILLIAM H. KELLEY NOTEBOOK
(COURTESY LIBRARY- ARCHIVES, REORGANIZED CHURCH OF JESUS CHRIST OF LATTER DAY SAINTS, THE AUDITORIUM, INDEPENDENCE, MISSOURI; COMPARE *SAINTS' HERALD* 28 [JUNE 1881]: 161–68)

[page 1] Dr. Stafford Rochester [lives] near Genisee Call Monger Street - Knows of the Latter day Saints Anthony Pratt in Manchester knows of them Thomas H. Taylor. we met in Manches[ter]. Was with John Brown. Says Smith [was] ducked in the creek in Manchester They did nothing Says nothing had been sustained against Smith

[page 2] Mary Bryant Born 1806 Says Cowd[e]r[y]s "were low Shacks." Cowd[e]r[y]s did not [join] Baptist Church or Methodist. Wm Brryant b[o]rn 1795. Says Smith was a drun[k]ard, but never saw him drunk. Says he remembers seeing Smith, but says he never saw him drunk. He knew nothing of the fam[i]ly on[ly] what was based on rumor. One he was acquainted with of the Smiths was [18]25 or [18]30 Mrs. Robinson of Jackson Mich-[igan] lives with Mr. Withy. She lived at Mormon Hill. [back of page 2] made these visits March 6 1881

[page 3] D. Booth Says O[liver]. Cowdry was a low pettifogging lawyer & Mason. guess he was no church member and Mason. Was Cowd[e]ry a drunkard[?] Every body drank then. Cowd[e]ry [was] known as ["]loos[e] Cowdry" Orin Reed Ezry Pierce lives in the Smith Neighborhood [back of page 3] Orland[o] Sanders lives on the Road leading from Palmyra to Manches[ter] Wallace Minors Dorius Peirce lives in Chesea Mich[igan]. Able Chase on Palmyra and Manchester Road

[page 4] Ezra Peirce. Says Joes did not know anything more about Hyglyerics Lyman Cowd[e]ry was a lawyer. O[liver]. Cowd[er]y [was a] School Teacher. Characters good. ["]I know that Joe Smith

was ignorant." Has pulled sticks with Joes for a gallon of Brandy but never knew [him] to get drunk. Born 1806.

[page 5] Orin Reed Lived in time of Smiths. in Town of farmington. I know nothing about the Smiths only by hearsay. [back of page 5] Major G[i]lbert of Palmyra sat up the type of B[ook]. of M[ormon].

[page 6] Orlando Saunders Say 78 year old in April Smiths worked for him and they were good fellows to work Hyram and the old man were coopers very good people. Every bod[y] drank in those days and the Smith[s] drank also. but they never got drunk. They were the best family in the neighborhood in case of sickness. One was at my house nearly all the time when my father died. Martin Haris was one of the first ones of the Town

[page 7] Able D. Chase 67 years old. Old man Smith was a cooper Alvin was the oldest ____ 6 boy[s] 2 girls - &c Alvin Hyr[um] - Josep[h] [Samuel] Harrison Wm & Carlos. Every one drank. I was young and don[']t remember only general character - poorly educated - ignorant and selfish - supersticious Shiftless but do a good days work. - Soby Joe - [back of page 7] E B Graanden printed B[ook]. of Mormon Whitmers went from Senaca Co Dr. [Philastus] Hurlbert lives at Coneaut. Ohio

[page 8] Jo[sep]h [Smith] got a s[ingular?] looking stone which was dug up out of my fathers well ____ [A?] Sister that [had] a stone she could see in, but it was not the one that Smith had Jackway) Hyram
                    Jessie

[page 9] Colonel John H Gilbert Sat up B[ook] of M[ormon]: Says he changed nothing about it. He punctuated it. Hyrum Brought Manuscrip[t] 24 Sheets at a time - B[ook]. of M[ormon] was commenced to be printed in August 1829 - and finished in March 1830 Lorenzo Saunders says [Sidney] Rydon was in the neighborhood befor[e] B of M was published 18 months Lorenzo

Saunders lives in New Adr[i]an Mich[igan]. [back of page 9] James L. Cob[b] of Salt Lake [City] corresponds with Colonel Gilbert.

[page 10] He knew Lyman and Oliver [Cowdery] Lyman was a petifogge[r]. Oliver was a school teacher - [Martin] Harris was a very honest farmer but very supersticious - He saw the Book with his spiritual eyes. 79 years of age.

[page 11] Hyram Jackway 65-6 Saw Joe and his Father Drunk in a hay field. Knows nothing about them stealing. Stafford was a Sailor. Wm Stafford He was the one that furnished the Black Sheep. ____[?] Smiths translated in the farm hous[e]. Maj Gilbert said they translated in a cave

[page 12] Hyram and his Father owed Mr. Jaynes 150$ Martin Harris was an honest man Harrison was a good worker for one day or a month. There were 6 boy[s] and 3 girls: The old lady Smith was kind in sickness. Cowd[e]rys good as the general run. Mrs. Jayn[e]s says [Pomeroy] Tucker never asked Willard Chase about what he knew

[page 13] John Stafford He [Joseph Smith] was a real clever jovial boy - What [Pomeroy] Tucker said about them was false absolutely - My father was never connected with them in any way - Smiths with others were hunting for money previous to obtaining plates My father Wm S- had a stone which some [back of page 13] thought they could look through - and old Mrs. S[mith]. came there for it but never got it. - 76 years old - Common then for any body to have drink in field those days one time Joe while working for some one on[c]e after he was married They had boiled cider Joe came in with his shirt torn - his wife felt bad about it & when they went

[page 14] home. She put shawl on him - had not been fighting - he was a little contentious but never saw him fight - known him to scuffle - Do a fair days work if hired out to a man but were poor managers. I lived a mile from them - My father is said to

have furnished a sheep - but I don[']t think my father was there at time they say sheep was [back of page 14] sacrificed - Cousin Christopher Stafford Aburn Geauga Co. Ohio, Oliver Cowd[e]ry Taught school in house 3 1/2 miles from Palmyry - Cowd[e]ry good Character. [Martin] Harris not very religious before B[ook] of M[ormon] - Was an Honorable farmer. Don[']t know whether he was sceptical or visionary - old Joe claimed he

[page 15] understood Geology and could tell all kinds of minerals - & they fixed up a dose for him. Joe was quite illit[erate] - until after they began to have school at at their house - they had school at their house. and studied their Bible - think Sidney R[igdon]. might have been there for the reason I can't account for the manuscript [Book of Mormon?] in [back of page 15] any other way - Don[']t know that Sidney was ever there before Book [of Mormon] was published. Sidney was never there that [Philastus] Hurlburt or [Eber D.] Howe or [Pomeroy] Tucker Could find out - Have been thinking and [hearing] about it for the last 50 years. Saw them dig 3 or 4 years before B[ook of Mormon] was found - Joe not there - The

[page 16] neighbors use[d] to Claim Sally Chase Could look through [a] stone she had & find money - Willard Chase use[d] to dig when she found where the money was Peaceable among themselves - old woman Had a great deal [of] faith [that] their Child[ren] - was going to do something great.

Index

M

M'Kune, Hezekiah, 152, 14
M'Kune, Joshua 73n, 115, 151
Mahaffey, J. E., 19
Mather, Frederic G., 4, 70, 95
Methodist, 73n, 153
Meyer, Eduard, 7
Michigan, 78, 87, 170
Millard, Asahel, 149
Miner, Wallace, 49-51, 170
Mitchell, Dr., 132
Murphy, Henry, 160
Murphy, Jack, 160

N

Neely, Albert, 69
Nibley, Hugh, 6-8, 11-22, 27-28, 109, 114
Nichols, Roswell, 34, 139-40
Nobles, J. K., 74n, 157, 158
North, Linus, 149

O

Orr, Robert, 166

P

Parke, Wm., 148
Payne, Hiram, 149
Payne, Samantha, 104n
Pearse, Darius (also Dorius, Pierce), 169, 170
Pennsylvania, 46, 69, 95, 109, 122-24,
Pierce, Ezra, 90-91, 170
Presbyterian church, 153
Purple, W. D., 74n
Putnam, Mr., 133

R

Reed, Amanda, 78, 90, 101n
Reed, Orin, 77-78, 90, 92, 100n-101n, 170, 171
Reed, Warden A., 147
Reynolds, George, 8n
Rice, Josiah, 148
Rigdon, Sidney, 80, 81, 87, 88, 154, 155, 159, 163, 171, 173
Risley, Mrs., 167
RLDS, 3, 75, 83

Roach, Rev. James B., 15, 151
Robinson, Clark, 148
Robinson, E. D., 149
Robinson, Mrs., 170
Rockwell, Mrs., 166, 168
Rockwell, Orrin Porter, 40n, 165, 167
Rogers, Joseph, 160-62
Rogers, Thomas, II, 146, 148
Rupert, Peter, 160

S

Saunders, Lorenzo, 46, 47, 80, 81, 86, 87, 88, 98, 162-63, 171
Saunders, Orlando, 94, 95, 98, 103n, 170, 171
Sawyer, Henry A., 67, 68, 164
Sexton, P., 149
Seymour, S. P., 149, 157
Sherer, John, 73n, 74n
Shook, Charles A., 17-18
Skinner, Jacob, 70
Smith, Alvin, 44, 47, 116, 122, 135, 166
Smith, Calvin, 156, 157
Smith, Carlos, 166, 168, 171
Smith, Catherine, 165, 166, 168
Smith, Emma Hale , 47, 61n, 128, 122, 124-25, 131-32, 156, 158-59, 169, 172
Smith, Frederick, 29, 126, 142
Smith, Hyrum, 45, 62n, 67, 79, 85, 108, 120, 125-26, 145, 147, 152, 153, 157, 164, 166, 168, 171, 172
Smith, Joseph, Jr., 1, 151, 167; Book of Mormon, 55, 119, 129-31, 134-38, 136, 153, 157, 172; drinking, 16-17, 67-68, 70, 82, 86, 91-92, 94, 107-108, 110n-11n, 140-42, 148, 154-55, 166, 171, 172, 149; money digging, 12-13, 18-21, 34-35, 39n-40n, 48-58, 67-68, 94-95, 118-19, 120-29, 131-32, 141-44, 155-57, 160-61, 164, 167-68, 172, 173; sheep story, 48-55, 145, 168, 173, 172; stone peeping, 43-48, 74n, 70, 109, 149, 154-55, 171; stealing, lying, 92, 97-98, 119, 143, 151, 161; youth, 153, 158, 173; women, 149, 158
Smith, Joseph, Sr., 24n, 23n-24n, 53-55, 61n, 62n, 98-99, 108, 121, 135-36,